A

WINNING THE WAR

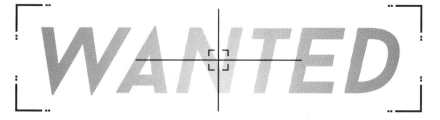

AGAINST YOUR SOUL

MAN

A

WINNING THE WAR

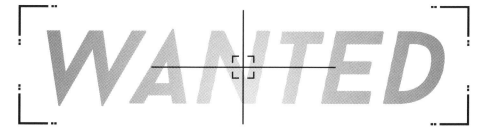

AGAINST YOUR SOUL

MAN

JASON CRUISE

SHILOH RUN PRESS

An Imprint of Barbour Publishing, Inc.

Member of the
Evangelical Christian
Publishers Association

CONTENTS

To my sons Cole and Tucker,

I have no clue why God chose me to be the man given the sobering honor of having you as my sons. Your talent, honor, and heart often leave me speechless. Watching you grow up before me, it is beyond question that you are rare young men who are going to be valiant Kingdom leaders. May you be eternally brave, fear nothing, and yet never forget that you have an enemy eager for your demise.

Stay forever sharp. I'll be with you, at the ready, to the very end. I promise.

—Dad

INTRODUCTION:
YOU ARE BEING HUNTED

Hated. Despised. Pursued.

That's who you are.

You have an enemy. He cannot kill you, for only God holds the keys to life and death.

He can, however, most certainly bring about the death of your heart. His idea of a pleasant evening would be to rip out your lungs with a dull knife and watch you die a slow and painful death. In light of the fact that he cannot kill you, he will gladly settle for crippling you with job loss, divorce, shame, bankruptcy, or even jail time.

This isn't fiction.

It's a reality you live every day. This hostile environment surrounds you like the air you breathe.

You don't have to believe it. In fact, don't believe it.

Don't believe it at all. Don't believe that you have an enemy. Just smirk at it and keep moving through your day.

He likes it that way.

Just realize that it's only a matter of time until you do actually believe it.

In that moment—when you are standing mere inches from your wife as she stares at a blurry, distorted image of your face because she's looking at you through tear-saturated eyes—remember that you didn't believe it. In all of your talking, in all of your explaining, just remember that she cannot hear your words, for your voice is echoing off the walls of her mind as it spins with the shock and pain you just inflicted on her.

That brutal fact is this: you are being hunted.

In that cold, quiet moment when you are losing your job and packing your pens, that golf trophy from the charity classic your team won last year, and your phone charger into a white banker's box—you know, the kind with handles cut into the sides—while the rest of your coworkers are watching but trying not to stare, remember that you didn't believe it.

When you literally cannot breathe because you can see in your son's eyes that he has questions screaming in his young mind—*What is going to happen to my family? Are we going to have to move? Is Daddy going to live here anymore?*—in that moment, my brother, you are going to believe it.

In that moment, when everything else about your life is foggy and dense and heavy, you will discover one truth so clear, so perfectly crisp, so clean—like a blue sky on a cloud-less winter day—you will know that you have an enemy.

And you're going to wish you'd confronted the most vital brutal fact a long, long time ago.

That brutal fact is this: *you are being hunted.*

By Satan

*Before you read any further, go to JasonCruise.com/
WantedMan and watch "The Story of Brian Hinkle."
Then come back and start reading from here.*

WHY THIS BOOK?

I'll never forget the day Brian called me. When I answered the phone, his trembling voice sounded weak.

"Brian, what's wrong?" I asked.

All he could say was, "I messed up. Real bad. I don't know what to do."

Later on, when I left Brian's house that day, my soul felt tired. It was a feeling I hadn't encountered in a long time. I just felt weary.

I've been weary before, true. Yet I couldn't remember a time when I experienced weariness from a battle I wasn't fighting personally.

Typically when your soul is tired, it's from being in a fight that has an impact on you personally. Your mom has cancer, so you walk with her and your dad through the oncology gauntlet. Your teenage daughter is crying because boys are not paying attention to her. You pray with her and for her for months on end, about her identity in Christ, and your soul is fatigued because she has your DNA. Those types of battles make sense. You should be tired from that kind of fighting.

With Brian, it was different.

I drove my truck out of his driveway, and I was over it. I mean, just fed up and over it. I felt so incredibly sick and tired and sick of being tired from watching brother after brother, men whom I truly loved, just getting their teeth knocked in from doing battle with the devil—or from *not* doing battle with the devil as they should.

What is going on? I found myself asking my own soul.

Yes, I knew it was Satan. Yes, I know we live in a spiritually hostile world. That wasn't my concern.

What I could not grasp is *why*. Why are so many men, later in life, like after forty, still falling to the very same enemies they fell to when they were young men in their twenties?

If a twenty-three-year-old guy has sex with his girlfriend, we chalk it up to him being a walking hormone, and in our minds, his age alone is at the core of the reason he did it.

At forty-two, I and my friends should know better, right? Yet all around me, I kept seeing man after man after man falling.

Some were losing jobs from falling to toxic levels of

arrogance and their unwillingness to be coachable or to grow professionally.

Some were falling to addiction.

Some were chained in depression and felt hopeless.

Some were falling to porn.

Some were falling to greed and the lust for a fat bank account.

Some were destroying their lives with unyielding bouts of anger.

About the time of the Brian Hinkle saga, men all around me were falling.

This one thing I knew: I was next.

THE SOBERING REALITY OF BEING ON THE HIT LIST

I wasn't next because I was wrapped up in living a double life. I wasn't next because I was pursuing ill-gotten financial gain. I was moving through manhood "okay," I suppose.

I knew I was most likely next, because on many fronts men I shared brotherhood with were taking sniper fire from the enemy, and I certainly wasn't exempt. When you walk around in sniper territory, you're going to be shot at; and I knew it was only a matter of time before I got hit.

Brian Hinkle's fall jolted me. Hard.

I felt as if I'd been hit by a stun gun, for a brother close to me had fallen—had taken a round to his heart spiritually. That one shot from the enemy had been well planned and tactically orchestrated. And while it was Brian who had been shot at, that solitary projectile had ballistic casualties far beyond him. His wife was wounded, his parents absorbed some of the pain from the shock of it, and so did his two sons. His friends felt the blow. His church also took some impact from the blast.

> *I knew I'd just been painfully reminded of this brutal truth: this land is not my homeland.*

I cannot tell you exactly why Brian's fall hit me so hard, other than that we were close. His fall caused in me a chain reaction of thoughts and feelings that had perhaps been dormant for a while.

When Brian went down, it became painfully evident to me that I was living, walking, networking, and operating as an alien in a foreign, hostile land.

Upon pulling out of Brian's driveway, with my heart on the floorboard of my truck, I knew I'd just been painfully reminded of this brutal truth: this land is not my homeland.

THE BRUTAL FACTS

The greatest, most effective leaders I know are readers. Leaders are readers; they learn early that they must never stop learning. My life has been changed by many books, mostly by faith-based leaders writing about what it means to live, walk, and survive in Christ as a man pursuing biblical manhood.

Every book that God has used to change my life is one that I've read more than once. I keep returning to certain books like a person would return to a freshwater well.

This trend holds true in my life with Jim Collins's globally famous work *Good to Great: Why Some Companies Make the Leap. . .and Others Don't*. While I'm not the world's strongest businessman, I enjoy knowing about business, for all of us are in business on some level. Instead of writing his arbitrary thoughts on how to win in business, Collins decided to research great businesses throughout history.

For example, Kroger and A&P sold groceries. Ask people born before 1970, and many of them will tell you, "Oh yeah, I remember A&P. My family shopped there all the time."

In Collins's mind, both Kroger and A&P sold the same stuff—toilet paper, soap, hamburger, and fruit. Virtually no differences existed, from a product perspective, between the two companies. So why, then, did A&P, this giant in the land of grocery stores, go bankrupt while Kroger is still alive today? In a word: *worldview.*

Good to Great isn't a book on business models as much as it is about how great business leaders think. And that got my attention.

Learning the fine points of interpreting profit-and-loss statements means nothing to me, but how great leaders think—well, that has massive value for me. So I found myself reading and rereading Collins's book over the years.

Perhaps the greatest truth I have taken away from Collins and his research on great corporate cultures is this axiom in the fourth chapter:

Confront the brutal facts (yet never lose faith).[1]

Why does this mean so much to me? Because I'm an optimist. I am that guy saying, "Yes, we can win, no matter what."

However, I also know that living in Utopia is often not as important as living in Realville.

In looking at why so many companies fail, Collins found that many leaders had charisma but their charisma was sometimes misleading. Not misleading so much in terms of being deceptive with employees, but in terms of having a "pie in the sky" mentality of leadership based not on numbers and trends but on blind hope.

Here's the truth: hope is not a strategy.

As Christian men, we can't just hope our way through living out godly manhood. It won't work. We need to have a biblical plan for winning.

> *We need to have a biblical plan for winning.*

Collins and his researchers found, in his own words:

"All good-to-great companies began the process of finding a path to greatness by confronting the brutal facts of their current reality. When you start with an honest and diligent effort to determine the truth of your situation, the right decisions often become self-evident. It is impossible to make good decisions without infusing the entire process with an honest confrontation of the brutal facts."[2]

1 : BRUTAL FACT #1
CONFRONT THE HUNT

Before you read any further, watch "Brutal Fact #1:
Confront the Hunt" at JasonCruise.com/WantedMan.

The brutal facts start with accepting the simple reality that you are being hunted. Operatives are out to get you, and they come in all forms.

The form they take is custom-designed to fit your personality, for deceivers are craftsmen. Never forget that.

ARX AXIOM

Arx axiom is a Latin concept meaning "the fortress of first principles."

Before you find victory—a true, sustainable victory in this journey of manhood—you must come to grips with one single principle: you must confront the fact that you are being hunted.

My grandfather, Joshua Lowrey Cruise, was five feet ten inches tall, yet he was larger than life in my eyes. I called him "Dat-Dat." I think "Dat-Dat" came from me not being able to say "Granddad" as a toddler, and as I grew older, it got shortened to "Dat."

Dat fought in World War II. Raised in the hills of Tennessee during the Great Depression, he grew up poor, never leaving his county until the day he received his draft card in the mail to go defend his country against the Nazis.

During his tour of duty, Dat's boots ran across Normandy Beach and all throughout Europe.

I didn't need movies like *Band of Brothers* or *Saving Private Ryan*, for Dat would dispense real-life stories in small doses over the years as time allowed him to talk about the things he'd witnessed.

Because of Dat's fighting in World War II, the European theater of war has forever been of interest to me. Often when a college professor assigned a paper, I'd write on something about that war, that era, or the political situations surrounding it.

One of the great truths I learned about the D-Day epic saga was that the war was actually won on that day. Any historian will tell you that one day changed world history forever.

Yet the reality was this: the war was won at Normandy, but the battle remained. The battle had to go all the way to Berlin before the war actually ended.

YOUR VERY OWN ARX AXIOM

The first principles of the war you're in now are no different. If you are a believer in Christ, the war you face was won the day Jesus came out of the grave. The battle, however, is recurring for the rest of your life until you meet Him face-to-face.

The context of the battle may change, but the fight remains to the very end.

> *If you are a believer in Christ, the war you face was won the day Jesus came out of the grave.*

THE FOUNDATION FROM HERE FORWARD

This book, *A Wanted Man*, came out of my investigation of a solitary verse—John 10:10.

Get this verse down. Know it in your mind, word by word, phrase by phrase. Seriously. Know it beginning to end. This verse is vital for living life smack in the middle of a manhunt.

(Satan)

"The thief comes only to steal and kill and destroy; I came that they may have life, and have it abundantly."

JOHN 10:10

If you isolate this verse and let it sink into your bones, you can feel the weight of it almost immediately. It took hold in my life through something quite unexpected.

I began to study the Gospel of John, and as I was reading it, this verse resonated through the annals of time and came at me almost from the scriptures themselves. With weight.

I turned this verse over and over in my head for weeks, even months.

It soon became apparent to me that a thief stalked me. Look, I knew that already. That was no new news.

However, I found his intent sobering. The discipline, the passion, the nonstop push the enemy had for me. And that's why I'm telling you we must break this verse down together for it to grab hold of our spirits.

IMAGINE THIS

Imagine you get a text message today that simply reads:

> I'm coming to kill you. Not today—but soon.

That single text message would alter the course of your

life, right? You'd be calling the police, and if they labeled it a serious threat, they'd probably bring in the FBI or at least state-level authorities to investigate.

You'd tell all of your closest friends. You'd let your employer know about it.

If you got that text and you didn't own a gun, you'd buy one before supper.

For reasons beyond me, John 10:10 confronted me. It wouldn't leave my mind. I'd read it a hundred times, but this time it took root.

I realized I would be in a battle for the rest of my life.

Daily you and I are being hunted. And if you expect to come out on the other side of this battle as a victor who is, as Paul said, more than a conqueror through Christ who loves us (see Romans 8:37), then you have to take Jesus' words in John 10:10 seriously.

KNOWING YOUR ENEMY

*For our struggle is not against flesh and blood,
but against the rulers, against the powers,
against the world forces of this darkness,
against the spiritual forces of wickedness
in the heavenly places.*
EPHESIANS 6:12

Just look at the visual language here in Ephesians 6:12: *struggle. . .flesh. . .blood. . .powers. . .forces. . .darkness.*

Those are war metaphors, descriptors of steel and grit and straight-up hand-to-hand combat. And Jesus understood those terms when He spoke of the "thief" in John 10:10.

In fact, Jesus didn't just confront the war at hand. He confronted the one *behind* the war. He knew the nature and the heartbeat of the enemy.

Jesus spoke with authority on the nature of the devil, and while I have no desire to go into a theology of the demonic, you need to know a few basic truths—arx axiom, a few first principles—that set the stage for the upcoming conversations you and I will be having about life as a wanted man.

You must first know *why* Jesus chose these metaphors of sheep, a shepherd, and a thief as found in John 10.

Jesus was illustrating life in the real world. He lived in the real world, and His stories, illustrations, and knowledge of life all made sense to the scores of people who encountered Him daily in that world in that time.

Think about it: Has it ever struck you that before Jesus went out on His journey as the Messiah, He first was part owner in a small business? Jesus had a profit-and-loss statement. He knew market rates and cost of goods sold. He knew what it meant to have customers with unrealistic expectations.

> *If you know the enemy and know yourself, you need not fear the result of a hundred battles. If you know yourself but not the enemy, for every victory gained you will also suffer a defeat. If you know neither the enemy nor yourself, you will succumb in every battle.*
> —SUN TZU, THE ART OF WAR

When a pretty girl walked past the carpenter shop, do you think Jesus turned His head in admiration? I do.

Was He a man? Yes, a man without sin, but a man none-theless. And that's the part about Jesus that some evangel-icals have never really been able to work through mentally. Myself included. It is tough to see Jesus as a man—a man like me. A man who needs deodorant. A man who gets blisters on his hands from working or a headache from pollen. How did He manage life in the same real world as I do—and never sin?

It's baffling—yet true.

So when Jesus used this metaphor of a thief, a shep-herd, and sheep, it was the perfect illustration for how life worked back then. It would have been no different than you starting out a story by saying, "So I grabbed my iPhone and asked Siri. . ." Everyone would know the context of your example.

In John 9:40-41, just before Jesus went into the "thief" illustration where He warned us that we are all wanted men, He gave up some information about the nature of the enemy. He did it in such a way, however, that those opposed to Him in the crowd—the religious Pharisees—could listen in as He actually talked about *them* to the people He was warning about this "thief" and his agents.

Just as the thief (Satan) and his agents (Pharisees) formed a militant group coming after the hearts and minds of everyday people in Jesus' time, so they and the messaging they use are still around today.

They just look different than they did back then.

THE SIN JESUS DESPISED

If there was one mind-set, one worldview, that Jesus simply all-out despised, it was the self-righteous arrogance of the religious elitists called Pharisees.

Jesus seemingly never missed an opportunity to pick a fight with these guys. He'd call out their hypocrisy in public. He never dodged an opportunity to expose their toxic approach to life, for their toxicity flowed out to thousands of people around them. They held hostage the liberating truths about the nature of His Father, and that angered Jesus.

Pharisees were the high-brass religious consultants of their day, devoted to leading people, but their destination for those people was nothing short of spiritual oppression.

Pharisees turned the spiritual journey into a difficult uphill climb. Rocky. Bitter. Impossible.

They made God out to be a cosmic accountant keeping up with debts owed and credits made. God was mysterious and hard to please, and evidently, by their standards, obsessed with depressingly trivial things like how many steps a person could take on a Sabbath day before it was considered work.

These religious agents, the Pharisees, made up the rules. And they enforced them, too. Pretty great position to be in, if you ask me, in terms of guiding culture.

To use Jesus' words, they would "tie up heavy burdens and lay them on men's shoulders, but they themselves are unwilling to move them with so much as a finger" (Matthew 23:4).

In Jesus' day, Pharisees were half-truth agents, expounding false religious teaching laced with some level of truth that seemed just familiar enough to the human heart to weigh it down.

While it may not make sense to you in a smartphone world, these religious authorities carried a monumental amount of street credibility.

I get the sense from reading the New Testament that these men were despised on some levels while revered on others. They were held in high esteem because it appeared as if they lived a life righteously set apart, but they were self-righteously arrogant. They were givers of money, but they snobbishly made sure others knew they gave it.

Jesus knew that these religious leaders didn't really care about people coming to know God and developing a relationship with Him. In other words, they weren't shepherds who cared about their "flocks."

So He capitalized on some easy branding while telling a story in a mixed crowd and drew a mental picture everyone could relate to: shepherds. These were rural people listening in, so He used that to His advantage.

You'd likely never talk about the use of a CASE tractor and all its farming implements to a group of NASDAQ brokers, right? Of course not. If you're a master communicator, you stick with the culture.

In Jesus' day, shepherds were all around.

People had to deal with both shepherds and sheep constantly. If you walked through a village marketplace, sheep would be somewhere nearby. You could hear them. See them. Smell them. Shepherds were in the marketplace, too, doing commerce often. I'm guessing you could smell them, too!

> *If you're a master communicator,*
> *you stick with the culture.*

One thing the locals knew about shepherds was this: they remained unquestionably committed to their sheep. They walked with them. Talked to them. Loved them. Protected them.

There was something savagely tender about a shepherd. He eased gently through life, walking the hillsides, but without remorse he'd kill a predator intending to mess with the flock.

> *"I Am the rule. So there are no more rules other than Me. Righteousness is found in a relationship with Me."*

Pharisees didn't protect anybody.

Jesus saw Pharisees the way shepherds saw wolves or wild dogs. Like predators, Pharisees were there to do harm, and they lived smack in the middle of daily life.

They kept the masses bound up in religious systems that kept them from a relationship with the God who made them.

Don't miss this. . . .

Pharisees thought finding God meant keeping the rules. "Keep the rules; keep God on your side" was their message. Remove the rules, and they literally didn't know what to do.

For a Pharisee, the rules were the relationship.

Then, seemingly out of nowhere, along comes this man from Nazareth, and He basically says to them, "Okay, fellas, let's make a new rule, and here it is: I Am the rule. So there are no more rules other than Me. Righteousness is found in a relationship with Me."

SOUTHERN CHRISTIANITY

I live in the South. We are nice down here for the most part. We speak to people we don't even know. No matter how educated Southerners may be, we say "y'all" and we all say "ain't," because those words just work.

People outside the South make fun of us all the time, yet I ask you, where does everyone come to retire? Case. In. Point!

One big problem with the South, at least when it comes to how we view Jesus, is that we've often mistaken discipleship for behavior modification—that is, be good, be nice, don't cuss, don't drink.... In other words, God favors good, clean living. So what has happened in the South over the last seventy-five years is that being a good, clean American citizen is basically the same thing as being a good Christian.

And that's a lie that comes straight from the pit of hell itself.

Why? Because you simply don't need Jesus to be good.

Having Jesus in your life certainly helps you to be good, but being good is not anywhere the same as being godly.

Pharisees were most certainly good citizens, but they were far from godly.

So when the Nazarene came along with a new message about rule keeping, Pharisees could not relate.

Obviously this was catastrophic to their society and religious culture. So catastrophic, actually, that I think most of today's evangelicals don't truly understand it in terms of how Jesus related to the Pharisees.

When Jesus took the rules off the table, Pharisees didn't know what to do. They now had to deal with the reality that their rule keeping was not the way to please God. Their guidelines for separating the sheep from the goats were now null and void.

They couldn't use their old measuring stick to sort out exactly who in society was a God follower and who wasn't. So when this messianic Messenger came along and said, "No more measurement apart from Me," their operational model immediately imploded.

So they had to kill the Messenger.

And that they did.

For three days anyway.

SMOKE SCREENS

Jesus said to Pharisees on one occasion:

*"You are of your father the devil, and you want
to do the desires of your father. He was a
murderer from the beginning, and does not
stand in the truth because there is no truth in
him. Whenever he speaks a lie, he speaks
from his own nature, for he is a
liar and the father of lies."*

J OHN 8:44

Right there—did you see that?

When talking to these Pharisees, the secret agents of Satan, Jesus gave insight about who they actually worked for—that is, He spoke of their employer.

Jesus gave some painfully clear and equally fascinating insights about the devil's nature. He knew the fallen angel "Lucifer," His enemy, well.

In John 8:44 Jesus used the words *murderer* and *liar* to describe him. He couldn't have talked about Satan like that if he was someone Jesus had never met!

The Pharisees were the oppressors, but they had a "money man." They were the operatives, but their employer stayed in the back channels. And Jesus saw right through that.

He called out their "father."

He was basically saying, "Look, I know you, and I know your daddy. You're just like him. I see right through your elitism and into your dirty selves; you're a bunch of soul thieves, just like your daddy."

Jesus made the point that these Pharisees were marketing agents for their daddy's corporate culture.

They had an agenda. As the voice of the enemy, they were shouting out all sorts of life principles to live by, and many people were listening.

(You can't miss that simple reality. People's lives were full of competing voices.)

Jesus, on the other hand, spoke of Himself as the "good shepherd" who lays down His life for His sheep (John 10:11). He could be trusted to lead humanity through rough terrain and eventually to heaven.

WHY DOES THIS MATTER?

You may be saying, "Okay, Jason, I get it. Pharisees were bad. Jesus was good. Why does this matter?"

This illustration from John 10—about a thief and his thieves and a good shepherd—is a story within an ongoing story.

Let me draw out a modern-day parallel about an employer and his employees. It's a story about the heart of the employer, his corporate culture, and the type of products being sold to the masses.

During Jesus' time on earth, the Pharisees were the media of the message, the voices calling out to the masses. They shaped the culture that people were engaging in every day.

Today, although the world doesn't seem to place much value on "religious" teaching, spiritual truths are nevertheless critical to life. So the enemy, the employer, has changed the branding. He's changed the sales pitch.

The products have also changed somewhat, but the enemy's motive has never changed. He's still trying to destroy you.

You are the target demographic. Everywhere you go, you are bombarded with messaging about *you*.

What *you* deserve.

What *you* should purchase.

Why *you* deserve luxury.

Why *you* should invest in this or why *you* should own that.

How many voices are competing for your loyalty every day?

That's what it is about: loyalty.

Your enemy Satan wants loyalty. He knows you'll never outright pledge loyalty to him.

Think about the last time you heard someone say, "Look, man, my allegiance is to Satan. He's why I do what I do." Only a few people who've ever walked the earth would say that outright.

Your enemy will let you be loyal to yourself. He'll let you demand your own way and do your own thing, because in the freedom to do your own thing, he knows that ultimately your loyalty will not be toward your heavenly Father.

MESSAGING SHAPES CULTURE

Have you ever thought about *who* is behind those voices and messages?

Have you ever thought about the values you value?

Have you ever thought about why you pledge loyalty to this philosophy or that one?

Have you ever thought about why you choose not to tithe and what you actually do choose to use your money for?

Have you ever thought about why you're raising your kids without discipline—that is, why you won't engage in biblical discipline but you'll listen to secular psychologists?

Have you ever thought about *why* you use a credit card for buying things you have no money to pay for, and what it says about how you view yourself?

> *Have you ever thought about the values you value?*

Do you see where I'm going?

Voices and messaging are all around, and if you think it's just product development, content marketing, and corporations doing what they do, you are naive, because. . .

Messaging shapes culture.

> *Messaging shapes culture.*

WHAT I'M NOT SAYING

I'm not saying that all of corporate America is evil.

I'm not saying that the devil is behind every billboard. That's not true at all.

I'm also not implying, in any fashion, that today's version of the Pharisees is the corporations, billboards, and marketing strategies that abound everywhere.

The connection is that Pharisees were the shapers of culture in that day, and they had a messaging or branding system that shaped the way people thought.

Besides looking different, nothing has changed much from that day to this: the thief is still the thief, and he still has messengers to carry his messages.

His agenda is the same: getting you to buy into something that will eventually take first place in your heart.

> *His agenda is the same: getting you to buy into something that will eventually take first place in your heart.*

"EVERY VIRUS NEEDS A SNEEZE"

Not long ago I was listening to a Seth Godin podcast.

If you are in any sort of business, you should know who Seth Godin is, because this guy is a freak of nature when it comes to talent. He's recognized by Fortune 500 companies as one of the greatest marketing minds on planet Earth.

I once heard financial guru Dave Ramsey say, "Seth Godin

lives in the future." Nothing could be truer. Seth Godin sees upcoming trends like nobody I've ever encountered.

I'd like to be a proper academician here and give the correct reference for the following quote, but truthfully it would take me a week to locate where I heard him say it or write it, because I've read several of his books and listened to many podcasts that featured him as a guest interviewee. So I'm just going to give credit here where credit is due.

I once heard Godin, when speaking on the concept of idea creation, say, "Every virus needs a sneeze."

This word image changed me on many levels. I write books, produce videos, and create media for men with the goal of bringing them closer to the God who made the dirt under their boots.

Men are visual—and Godin's metaphor was perfect for me. He was right. You can have the best idea ever thought, but if you cannot find a way to sneeze that sucker to the rest of the world, it honestly doesn't matter how good your idea is at all.

When I began thinking about Pharisees and enemies and thieves and flocks and people and cultures and how all of these tie together with messaging, I thought of Godin's analogy of viruses and sneezes.

The Pharisees were sneezing the ideas their "father"

was creating. And Satan is still sending out his deceptive messages today.

Like every other grassroots movement that has ever existed, messaging is only as good as the quality of distribution. The bubonic plague that ravaged the Middle Ages would have been totally harmless unless it rode out to the masses on a vehicle, which in this case was a bite from the rat flea.

In the John 10 era, Pharisees served as the agents Satan used to spread lies and deception. They were the vehicles that carried the message.

Today the lies are the same, but the messengers are different.

VOICES

That's what we are up against today. Messages. Voices. Noise from every corner that competes.

You must be aware of the culture you live in daily. You must realize that you are living in a society where everything at every turn is competing for your loyalty and attention.

Let me get ahead of something on this issue before you brush it off. . . .

JASON CRUISE

There's a boatload of men out there who carry the mentality, *I don't care about all of that. Those television ads, those radio spots, those banners that pop up on websites—I just ignore all that stuff because it doesn't affect me.*

> *You must realize that you are living in a society where everything at every turn is competing for your loyalty and attention.*

Really, it doesn't affect you?

Then you need to explain why corporations paid up to $5 million for a thirty-second ad during the 2016 Super Bowl to get your attention.[1]

Are the heads of those corporations stupid? Are those companies led by CEOs and marketing teams that are anti-intellect on every level?

No. You *are* able to be influenced. And while a beer commercial may not get to you, messages sink into your bones over time.

Many years ago I heard a leadership axiom that goes like this:

It takes up to a mile for a large battleship or aircraft carrier to make a U-turn in the ocean. So how do you turn a battleship? Constant pressure on a small rudder.

That's how the enemy, the thief, wins with his messaging. Constant pressure on your mind. Constant pressure speaking lies mixed with truths over the course of a few years, getting you to rethink things that once were nonnegotiables in your life.

Now consider that we are currently living in the most biblically illiterate culture we've ever seen.

Let's put it all together. We live in a culture rife with incredibly well-crafted messages everywhere. A culture where companies pay good money to get access to your purchasing habits so they can send you messages that appeal to your core values.

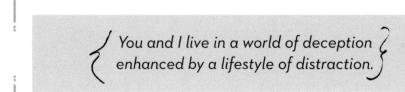

You and I live in a world of deception enhanced by a lifestyle of distraction.

Stack that sort of powerful, well-funded messaging up against the average person—including the average churchgoing person—who is biblically illiterate.

What do you get?

Sheep wandering around doing life in hostile territory.

That's what we're up against today, my brother.

You and I live in a world of deception enhanced by a lifestyle of distraction.

> ***There's the money voice.*** Financial Pharisees are constantly telling you, "Get that bigger house. You deserve it. You need it. We'll offer it to you at 3.1 percent. Never mind that you can't pay for it. Never mind that you have $22,000 of credit card debt already. You deserve a bigger house, and you can figure it out later."

> ***There's the identity voice.*** Messages on how to get ahead bombard today's workingman. Voices of corporate competition tell you that if you're not winning, you're losing. The enemy's marketing agents are always there, telling you to take more pride in your market value as a businessman. Pay attention and you'll start to notice

that there's just enough truth mixed with lies to keep you distracted from the Identity Giver.

There's the sex voice. Steadily creeping into your life are songs on the radio telling you that looking at her is nowhere near the same as touching her. It's a victimless action, so they say. Magazine ads linger in your periphery, hoping to get you to look at her cleavage for one extra second while you consider the product being sold. Thoughts are planted into your mind, and daily you must struggle to push them out.

I could go on and on and on and on.

Voices all around you, and every man responds to different voices in different ways.

Some men are honestly quite immune to porn, while others fall easily to it. Some men have a soft spot for money, while others aren't too concerned with wealth.

It doesn't matter to the devil. He has messaging built on design spec created just for you. Every virus needs a sneeze. The right kind of sneeze pointed at the right target.

People in Jesus' day knew this about sheep: sheep live outside the city in a hostile environment.

Every. Single. Day.

And Jesus tapped into that idea about a hostile world.

So the hunt was on then, and the hunt is on now. <u>And if you want to win, if you want to live, you'd better confront the hunt.</u>

> { *If you want to win, if you want to live, you'd better confront the hunt.* }

2 : BRUTAL FACT #2
YOU LIVE OUTSIDE THE WIRE

Before you read any further, watch "Brutal Fact #2: You Live outside the Wire" at JasonCruise.com/WantedMan.

"The thief comes..."

Haunting words.

Shepherds and their sheep lived outside the city in the rough country. Outside the city walls. Outside the wire.

Most cities in those days had walls. That's why Jesus, as well as the Old Testament writers, often made reference to "the city gate." These barriers were meant to keep out intruders.

Think of these gates as a modern-day umbrella policy you purchase from your insurance agent.

My insurance agent looks out for me.

Recently my wife and I added some investment property to our portfolio, and in reviewing the risks, my agent suggested an umbrella policy because my risk had become greater after increasing my net worth. Just as an umbrella policy protects everything under it, a city gate protected everything behind it. It was, as they say in the insurance world, "another layer of protection."

Shepherds and sheep lived outside the umbrella. They were exposed, which for them was the price of doing business. Everyone knew that shepherds lived vulnerable lives outside the gate, or wire, of protection.

My Special Forces buddy, Brad—whom I mentioned in the most recent video I asked you to watch—has told me a lot about the wireless life.

I'll never forget him talking about what it felt like to leave the security of the umbrella. He said that his team knew the Taliban or local militants were watching them.

Not only did they know it; they heard it. Immediately.

As soon as the gate went up, they heard increased chatter on their radio frequencies. Brad said they knew the moment their convoy left the wire that they were in the hot zone.

And that's why it felt so very stressful. Their senses

remained on critical high alert. They knew the chances of beings shot at or the likelihood of hitting an IED had just gone up dramatically.

LIFE TODAY AS A JESUS FOLLOWER

You are being hunted whether you like it or not. Jesus made it clear that the enemy is on the hunt. Walking toward you. Planning behind the scenes of your life. Talking about you. Watching you.

In John 10:10 Jesus made it painfully clear for you, my brother. Your enemy is real, and you are walking in his territory now. The thief is coming at you, and he is no ordinary enemy.

Your enemy is *the* enemy of enemies—the underlord of evil.

> *Your enemy is the enemy of enemies—the underlord of evil.*

Today the enemy is thinking about how to gain access to your children.

Today the enemy is thinking about your relationship with your boss.

Today the enemy is thinking about your sex life.

Today the enemy is thinking about you.

Every single facet of you is on his mind.

The day you gave your life to Christ, you actually made two decisions, and yet most likely you were aware of only one of them.

You gave your life to Christ. You felt elated. If your salvation experience was anything like mine, people praised you to high heaven. Teachers sent notes. Preachers sent words of affirmation. You'd walk into church and elders of the community would tell you how proud they were of you.

It was great. And it should be great. It's supposed to be great.

The problem comes in what many never told you: life is full of battles. Real battles. Epic battles. And some of them, you are going to lose. And when you lose, you're going to get wounds.

So, yes, the day you came to Christ, you made a decision. You also declared yourself an enemy to the devil. You

I don't want her parking next to just anyone in a parking lot. I tell her to look around at her situation and to walk out of stores with her head up, making eye contact with strangers.

Condition Yellow *is awareness*. Any person who teaches self-defense or tactical training can tell you about living in Condition Yellow. You can train yourself to live with this kind of awareness so that it becomes muscle memory.

Under Condition Yellow, you are alert, at least somewhat. You notice people's habits on some level.

For instance, you walk into a convenience store and notice two guys wearing hoodies with the hoods up over their heads. They may not be criminals, but they are together, and both are wearing hoodies; it's a bit suspicious. You simply need to take note of it.

I carry a gun. I've taken the required concealed-carry classes, but I've taken some advanced tactical classes as well. They were really worth it, too.

In my advanced courses, one of my instructors talked about the Cooper Code. He talked about training yourself with muscle memory because muscle memory kicks in big-time under pressure. People's repetitive responses when under distress are amazing.

My instructor gave us a few examples, but how to ap-proach convenience stores is one that has stuck with me to this day.

He taught us to get in this habit: as you walk up to the doors of the store after pumping gas, look at the counter *before* you go inside. Look to see if someone is standing at the counter or nearby.

Look to see if the clerk is standing really still, almost robotic in nature. Look to see if the person standing nearby has their head down, most likely wearing a hoodie.

If so, something might be up. It could be that the clerk is in the process of being robbed and the thief is just waiting on you to check out and leave.

That's situational awareness, and situational awareness is what keeps you alive, my brother.

Let me tell you just how critical to survival awareness can be. My instructor, who has become a friend of mine, had an encounter a few years ago that was truly ironic for someone who teaches situational awareness.

Ken is an active law enforcement officer who, as I said, also trains the average citizen in concealed carry and tactical response. In fact, he is often even brought in to teach local and state law enforcement. He is *that* good!

He was at the movies with his wife. She gets cold easily,

so during the movie she couldn't get warm, and he went out to the SUV to grab her coat.

Ken carries a gun 24/7. You simply are not going to find him unarmed. Protecting himself and others is a lifestyle, not a hobby. He knows the dangers of being unarmed, and he simply refuses to be a statistic.

I'll share the encounter in his own words. He said:

> *I noticed from a distance that three adult males were wearing hoodies and walking right at me. [They were] standing side by side and approaching me rapidly from about forty yards away. I changed direction, walked through some parking spaces, chose a new lane opposite them, put cars between us, and continued forward. No big deal.*
>
> *Nobody was in the parking lot. Just me and them.*
>
> *However, they did the same thing. They crossed through the lanes of cars and came over to my side, making direct eye contact with me. They continued to walk directly at me. Side by side. It was obvious they were going to rob me.*
>
> *At twenty yards away, I simply pulled out my gun, drew down at low ready, pointed just in front*

of them, and yelled out, "Can I help you fellas with anything?"

Upon seeing his weapon and hearing his question, they bolted!

Ken's commitment to situational awareness saved his life; actually, I'd say it saved the lives of the three guys. No kidding. They had no idea who they were up against! If Ken were to click off ten rounds, he'd hit his target with nine of them. Yet he avoided a gunfight, and they avoided sheer death at the hands of a man who wouldn't hesitate to end the threat.

Ken lives in a constant state of Condition Yellow, and in this particular situation he shifted into the next phase—Condition Orange—when the threat persisted.

Condition Orange *is being prepared to fight*. In Ken's encounter he moved from being aware that a threat could come to noticing a threat approaching, and once it escalated, he was ready to fight if necessary.

Condition Red *is fighting.* That is, the fight is on. It's time to survive at all costs.

SPIRITUAL AWARENESS

Ask any Christian male, and he'll readily admit to the power of evil; but watch how he operates daily, and you'll see a diminished response to that very same evil power he so readily acknowledges. Is that not perplexing?

Can you imagine being deployed to the Middle East to fight ISIS but living daily as if you were back at home walking your kids to ball practice?

Yet that is what most men do in terms of living life outside the wire.

The average Christian man walks around as if there's no real war going on around him. Sure, he'll admit there is a devil. Sure, he'll admit that evil is real and present, yet there's a mental disconnect to his willingness to admit that "the thief comes."

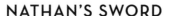

NATHAN'S SWORD

My inner circle consists of a few brothers whom God has provided to walk with me outside the wire. Our relationships are deep and filled with many layers that undergird our bond of brotherhood.

> *The average Christian man walks around as*
> *if there's no real war going on around him.*

One of those chosen few is a man named Pierce Marrs. Pierce is a world-class professional and a career coach. Most of all, he's a man of God. He's well read, and he pursues life.

Pierce and I have had lunch together only one time.

And that same lunch is still a monthly appointment. The reason we've had only one lunch is that the same lunch never ends. We just pick up where we left off. We never close the conversation; it just lingers until the next month when we pick back up and solve 87 percent of the world's problems, leave the 13 percent until the next time, and then do it again.

It's awesome. I never leave my perpetual lunch with Pierce without being a better man on every level, having gleaned from his heart and wisdom.

Pierce told me a story once that has never left me. It was about his youngest son, Nathan. Nathan is a grown man now and recently returned from China where he was serving as a missionary.

From his youngest years, Nathan loved film. Movies, drama, plotlines, character development—all those things resonated with Nathan. Pierce, being the career coach he is, would often exegete life with Nathan through films they'd watch.

Pierce told me that from the start, Nathan loved anything with battles and swords. Especially swords. Even to the point that as a young boy he would go out in the yard and practice sword maneuvers, actually becoming quite impressive with how he handled the blade.

One night during the early years when Pierce went up to tuck Nathan into bed, he noticed Nathan had put a sword by his bed.

"Son, I see you've got your sword. Why did you prop it up beside the bed tonight?" Pierce asked.

Nathan responded, "I just want to be ready, Dad."

Ready.

Think about that. Here's a young boy who doesn't want to be unprepared should the fight come his way. Nathan had something inside him that told him that life, his included, had villains within it. And he just wanted to be. . .ready.

We all live outside the wire, yet most of us live out there walking through minefields every day, eating a burrito and drinking a Coke. Readiness is not something we live by habit.

We are, in a word, _lulled_.

A WORLD OF DISTRACTIONS OR A WORLD OF DECEPTIONS?

Do we live in a world of distractions or a world of deceptions? I think it's both.

Jesus said that we are "not of the world" (John 17:16). That is, He understands that life is lived outside the wire—in hostile territory.

Talk with any military combat veteran, and he'll tell you that combat is a surreal emotional ride.

I had an older friend who saw intense combat in the Vietnam War. He said to me, "Combat is an odd daily grind.

Combat is twenty-three hours and forty-five minutes of the most mind-numbing boredom you can imagine, with fifteen minutes of panic and terror like you've never known before—and then it's over until you do it again later."

That's what I think about when I think of life outside the wire. We don't live unaware of the enemy, but we walk rank and file down the path of the redeemed knowing that our redemption is not complete just yet because we are still on this side of heaven. We know that we are in hostile territory, but we've learned to move on because in many cases we have small scars from the occasional wound. A wound that, while painful, is still manageable.

So we live with the lull, never thinking about the storm of combat that confronts us daily. Because the combat isn't loud, with bullets flying everywhere and bombs going off beside us, our senses are dulled; but that doesn't change the fact that combat exists where we live.

It's just not chaotic, or so it seems.

SET UP

Most of us, certainly myself included, never realize that we are being set up and pursued.

I believe that we are lulled into being comfortable with life outside the wire by living amid so many nonthreatening daily distractions.

Like me, you have a career path demanding a massive amount of your time and mental energy.

> *Most all of us live overloaded lives, in constant distraction, while navigating that very same life in occupied enemy territory.*

You may have kids, as I do. You love them dearly, and you are consumed with providing for them and keeping them on track. Like me, you live in a world where technology is overbearing. We call those little devices "mobile phones," but they are far from mobile, for we are chained to the tiny tyrants 24/7.

Try to see if you can walk away from life without a cell phone. Truthfully you could lose your job, because your employer might require that you remain accessible upon demand.

Push through the fog and see your life as you live it in this very moment.

Most all of us live overloaded lives, in constant distraction, while navigating that very same life in occupied enemy territory.

Now think about how easy it is for a thief, a robber, or an assassin to operate in a climate of distraction.

Operatives thrive in that environment, and some operatives are even known to create an environment of distraction to make their job easier.

Condition White is how the devil makes his money. He just keeps distracting you, often giving you what you want to make his job easier.

Life outside the wire means that every man who is "in Christ" lives, walks, and operates in hostile territory.

NAVIGATING LIFE OUTSIDE THE WIRE

In the past several years, I've learned a valuable truth: slowing down and camping out in a passage of scripture offers some of the most rewarding spiritual terrain I traverse.

When you're not in a hurry to move on, it's amazing what you see. As I said earlier, I have read and reread all the good books that have changed my life on some level.

It's mind-boggling to me what happens when I simply let one area of truth saturate my life over and over again. So I did that with the books of 1 and 2 Peter not long ago.

It was during duck season (I remember that for some reason). I would get up, fix some coffee about 5:00 a.m., and then for about an hour study this one section of scripture from Peter's pen, poring over it again and again.

Here's the driving key—the "secret sauce" that Peter was trying to get into his readers' heads: a Christ follower is a temporary resident in a foreign country.

Peter even started out his first letter trying to drill this idea into his readers by saying, "To those who reside as aliens, scattered throughout..." (1 Peter 1:1).

His audience contained a large number of messianic

Jews. Many of them were new Christ followers who had been pushed out of Jerusalem due to the persecution of Christians.

Don't miss this.

It is not a history lesson.

It's the ball game.

Understanding the historical background of Peter's letters is critical to understanding the groundwork of the enemy in your life today.

The Gospel was spreading. People following Jesus were being forced to recalibrate the gears in their heads on how to live everyday life.

Life as they knew it—life's traditions, life's flow, what they had been told to believe—all of it was changing. And now, to avoid being killed for their belief system, many were fleeing their homeland.

So Peter used words and phrases that only a traveler would understand. He spoke to them as fellow Jews, because Peter himself was a Jew. He spoke to them as a man who knew what it felt like to be persecuted for his beliefs, because Jews were persecuted then, and they still are now.

Imagine being brought up in a way of life that was now changing before your very eyes—as referenced in 1 Peter 1:17–18, where Peter said, "Conduct yourselves. . .knowing that you were not redeemed with perishable things like silver and gold from your futile way of life inherited from your forefathers."

Spiritually you're alive and you've found purpose in following Jesus, but you're paying for it, too.

Peter didn't sugarcoat this hard truth for his people. Some were messianic Jews and some were new Christians outside the Jewish tribes, yet all had come to faith in Christ, and they had to live out that faith in a spiritually hostile world.

So that's why we find Peter using words that could help his readers cope with persecution:

> 1 Peter 1:1—"aliens, scattered throughout"
> 1 Peter 1:13—"prepare your minds for action, keep sober in spirit"
> 1 Peter 1:17—"during the time of your stay on earth"
> 1 Peter 2:11—"I urge you as aliens and strangers"
> 1 Peter 4:1—"arm yourselves"
> 1 Peter 5:8—"be on the alert"
> 2 Peter 3:17—"be on your guard"

Col. Jeff Cooper perhaps took some cues from Peter for his Color Code for Readiness. We find Peter doing everything he could to encourage God's people to keep their minds alive and maintain perspective in a hostile world.

Look at what he wrote in 2 Peter 2:1–3, 17–19:

> But false prophets also arose among the people, just as there will also be false teachers among you, who will secretly introduce destructive here-sies, even denying the Master who bought them, bringing swift destruction upon themselves. Many will follow their sensuality, and because of them the way of the truth will be maligned; and in their greed they will exploit you with false words; their judgment from long ago is not idle, and their de-struction is not asleep. . . .
>
> These are springs without water and mists driven by a storm, for whom the black darkness has been reserved. For speaking out arrogant words of vanity they entice by fleshly desires, by sensuality, those who barely escape from the ones who live in error, promising them freedom while they themselves are slaves of corruption; for by what a man is overcome, by this he is enslaved.

Messages are all around, competing for your loyalty.
And that brings us to the question: Who is the author?
Who would be behind that sort of environment?
More importantly, what is this enemy after?

3 : BRUTAL FACT #3
THE POWER OF OBSESSION

Before you read any further, watch "Brutal Fact #3:
The Power of Obsession" at JasonCruise.com/WantedMan.

"The thief comes only..."

It came in a quiet moment for me. I had studied Jesus'
words on shepherds and sheep and hostile territory for
months, letting these truths sink in deep, and yet somehow
I'd overlooked it.

One simple word: *only*.

The thief isn't just active; his motive is crystal clear.

"The thief comes only to steal and kill and destroy" (John
10:10).

The devil has no other agenda. He is concerned with only

one thing: *bringing you down.*

The legendary theologian F. F. Bruce said it well: "The thief's designs on the sheep are wholly malicious; the good shepherd's plans for them are entirely benevolent."[1]

Jokes about the devil may be fun for late-night talk show comedians, but there's nothing comical about the reality of what the devil is doing when it comes to the subject of you.

> *The devil has no other agenda. He is concerned with only one thing:* bringing you down.

Shroud the devil's pursuits any way you want and wink at his schemes, but that will have no bearing whatsoever on how serious he is about destroying everything your life touches.

While you and I may live overloaded lives, Satan does not. He has one thing on his mind: you.

THE ORIGINAL TERRORIST

The devil doesn't hang out in full demonic form for all to see. No. He lives in the shadows, like bin Laden, operating his agents from the back channels. Satan is a terrorist who stays close but simultaneously just far enough away so as not to be recognized until the bomb goes off. Then he proudly takes credit while dancing in the street over your demise.

Many years ago I was listening to a US Army combat veteran talk about his experiences in the Middle East. He had seen several combat tours in the post–9/11 era while fighting global terrorism.

He said, and I'm quoting loosely here from memory—but a good memory—"For those Americans who hate the idea of us being in Iraq, Afghanistan, or having our troops deployed trying to liberate Kuwait, or doing whatever we do in terms of military operations in the Middle East at large—those dissenting Americans see our deployments as politically motivated oil wars. What most Americans never have seemed to understand is that for terrorists, this is not a political war. I learned that from being over there in combat. For them, it's a holy war. And they are not going to stop."

> *While you and I may live overloaded lives,*
> *Satan does not. He has one thing on his mind: you.*

Americans don't like the idea that anyone would hate us—I mean really, really hate us. We can't understand that.

It just doesn't make sense to the average American mind that someone would hate us so much that they'd want to kill us.

But I can promise you this: the devil wants you dead. Because he cannot control life and death, however, he must settle for carnage.

Therefore he is obsessed with wounding you. Deeply. Painfully. With scars to show as trophies.

OBSESSIONS

My dad hunted and fished, and he did both well.

Dad loved to hunt, yes, but hunting took on a different path for me. I became obsessed with it at an early age. Even when I was just ten, there wasn't anything about hunting I didn't love.

I loved the gear, the elements, the different weapons. Most of all I loved the pursuit. It was the chase that I craved the most.

The problem with hunting—or I should say, with hunting well—is that if you want to be good at it, it's a consistent process.

Anything you want to be good at can easily become an obsession. Those who are obsessed are driven, and driven individuals have resolve.

Growing up as a hunter, I knew the power of obsession from a young age. I watched some of my father's friends who were great hunters experience success upon success in terms of trophy bucks they took down year after year.

Big-buck hunters readily fit the description of the obsessed. They will tell you that they are planning tree stand arrangements, interception points, and food plots year-round. Big-buck hunters are scouting in March when trails are still easy to see. They are researching food-plot nutrition systems in early spring. They are determining which parts of their farms they will plant and which parts of their farms they won't even enter so as to provide deer sanctuary.

Then there's preparation.

Every solid bow hunter I know shoots his bow year-round on some level. In fact, my friend Max, who is by far the best bow hunter I've ever seen, shoots three to four arrows a day just for muscle memory. Every. Single. Day.

Max and I were on an elk hunt in Colorado years ago. We met up around noon at a predetermined vantage point so that we could walk down the mountain together. I asked him, "Max, how far would you shoot at a bull? I mean, if there weren't really high winds to deflect your arrow's trajectory, how far would you feel comfortable shooting knowing that you'd kill him?"

Max is a very humble and quiet man, but without even thinking about it, he said, "I wouldn't hesitate at seventy yards."

TALENT COMES FROM A RECKLESS OBSESSION TO BE THE BEST

And that's what you and I face with our enemy. He's obsessed, and because he's obsessed, he's talented.

He's the very best—the best who's ever existed—at ruining a man's legacy.

> *He's obsessed, and because he's obsessed, he's talented.*

He's toppled both the wealthy and the destitute without regard to stature. Coaches, players, politicians, priests, preachers, atheists, dads, granddads, students, professors, all men everywhere—those are his prospective clients. He has no prejudices or preferences about whom he wrecks. He pursues a vengeance devoid of mercy.

4 : BRUTAL FACT #4
EVERY GOOD THIEF IS BOTH
PATIENT AND INTENT

Before you read any further, watch "Brutal Fact #4: Every Good Thief Is Both Patient and Intent" at JasonCruise.com/WantedMan.

"The thief comes *only* to *steal* and *kill* and *destroy*" (John 10:10, emphasis added).

In looking at how the enemy pursues us, the idea of stealing, killing, and destroying is where obsession takes a turn. A turn for the worst.

It makes me think of the dog that chases your truck when you pass his home. He's lying in the front yard, sees you coming down the road, and stands up. You know what's coming.

He's going to chase after you and let you know that you'd

better not stop your moving hunk of metal in front of his lair.

Often I think to myself, *Ol' boy, what if you caught me? What if you just got lucky and latched on with that mouth of yours? What would you do with a mouthful of Tundra moving at fifty-seven miles per hour?*

In reality a yard dog has no clue what he'd do if he caught your vehicle. He's barking because that's what he does.

There's normally nothing behind it—no intent for harm, just harassment.

The same is not true of the devil.

He fully intends to catch you, and he knows exactly what to do with a mouthful of metal. Unlike a yard dog, he has a very real intent for collateral damage. He is out to steal, kill, and destroy—to take something important and of value from *you.*

What the devil and the yard dog do have in common is that both are patient and strategic in how they wait for their prey. A yard dog positions himself near the road—always. He wants the best sight line for an oncoming opportunity.

I've noticed over my years of driving familiar country roads that the same dog on the same road always lies down and waits in the same place for vehicles to drive by so he can do his deal once again.

It is here, my brothers, that I want you to open your eyes

and clear your minds, for this is where the average evangelical male has failed to connect the dots regarding how our enemy operates.

I am in my forties. Which means that, like you, I have been given the ignoble gift of watching many men fall to the enemy who pursues our hearts.

Many times I've met a guy for lunch or been asked to come to his office or to meet him somewhere off the beaten path discreetly so that we could discuss some failure in his personal life. In those times, as I thought through common denominators linking a man's failures, I began to see a trend—a simple reality that I just hadn't seen before until a few years ago.

> *I believe Satan's most misunderstood, unknown, truly secret weapon is this: patience.*

What I began to realize after hearing stories of failure from my brothers and colleagues was that none of their failures—*none of them*—happened overnight.

Stop for a second and let that sink in.

Please.

No man gets up one day and says to himself, *You know, today seems like a great day to hook up with another woman, get naked, have sex, ruin my marriage, destroy my family, and lose my job due to my life imploding.*

No reasonable man thinks or acts that way.

I cannot think of a single man I've had a conversation with who was navigating the aftermath of failure who actually could not, on at least some level, point back to a season in life when he knowingly began to sabotage his own journey.

I have asked many of them, "When did all of this start?" It blows my mind how specific they are with their answers. So many men I know can recall with vivid detail when they began the digression:

> *"It was when I took this new role at my job and started looking at her more than I should."*

> *"It was when I began to start drinking again, the night of a class reunion. That's when it all started to fall apart."*

> *"It was when I chose work over my wife that things began to slowly deteriorate."*

Time and time again, men have told me they can look

back and see the signs of being set up by their enemy.

I believe Satan's most misunderstood, unknown, truly secret weapon is this: patience.

NOBODY SEES THE DEVIL
AS AN ENEMY WHO IS PATIENT

Patience allows someone, a thief especially, to be creative.

I've heard many people over the years say, "I'm creative under pressure." I disagree. I've been a writer, speaker, and media producer for far too long to believe that anymore. People are not creative under pressure, because creativity takes time. People under pressure are simply good at improv.

They learn to improvise under pressure, but improv is not creativity.

This brings me to my point: only after resting on this verse for many months did something float to the surface of my heart. That's what happens when you marinate something: things soak in over time.

What rose to the surface was that a good thief rarely operates on impulse.

Notice I said *good* thief.

Think about it: What is a criminal's greatest fear? Being

imprisoned for his crimes.

Why would a good thief risk everything he's worked so hard to achieve by acting on impulse? In every documentary I've ever watched about actual career criminals, especially jewel thieves, they were men of great precision. I remember watching an exclusive on a jewel thief who robbed expensive homes in Florida. He went into great detail discussing how he would narrow down his search for families who had expensive jewels. He would research jewelers, find one who would take a bribe to give up information, and then get to work making a plan.

After watching the home for weeks, he would approach the cleaning staff and offer a staffer a huge amount of money for information on when the family typically ate dinner, when they were using one part of the house over another, and other minute details. Once he had the staff on the payroll, he would plan the heist.

He would actually access the house from the ocean! He would paddle in on a skiff to remain silent, much akin to a Special Forces operative.

Think for a second about the sheer magnitude of this guy's discipline. He could have been a super executive. I could see him thriving in honest work as a chief operations officer of a major corporation.

Consider what it must take to investigate the background

of a family, their staff, their habits, where they hang out, when they eat, and what times they leave and return home.

Think of the talent this thief possessed to be not only willing but also able to traverse the ocean in a skiff.

All of that energy, all of that creativity, all of that discipline—all poured into one idea: taking something of worth from a mark.

From that same interview, I remember how it struck me that the thief was incredibly risk averse. The one thing he said he wanted to avoid at all cost was contact with people. He was a burglar, not a rapist. He wanted to be in, out, and gone while leaving absolutely nothing to chance that might get him caught.

> *The devil is the master of setting you up over time for a battle that comes when you're weak.*

So he took his time and chose his jobs based on risk.

When it comes to wrecking people's lives, Satan is typically not into smash-and-grab jobs on the front end. He saves that for the finale. He plots. He plans. He sets you up time and time again. Then when he does strike, I've noticed it is often loud and fast.

In most cases, obsessions cause us to act rapidly with intensity and drive, but that's not how the devil operates. His obsession, while fully fueled, is often steady and slow. He is the master of setting you up over time for a battle that comes when you're weak.

THE SETUP AND HOW IT'S DONE

When I first started turkey hunting, I didn't know anything about killing a turkey. Now, I'd been a hunter pretty much since I was able to walk, but when I was growing up, turkeys were almost an endangered species in the South. The National Wild Turkey Federation began efforts with state wildlife agencies to bring the turkey back, but I was out of high school before I started frequently seeing flocks in the woods.

Needless to say, in those days access to information was beyond limited. When I started turkey hunting, our version of Google came in the form of a big brick building called a library!

This meant that if you wanted to learn to turkey hunt, you had to want to learn really, really badly—badly enough that you'd seek out wisdom. So that's what I did.

The single greatest resource of turkey knowledge I found, or have ever found, came in the form of two men from Kentucky: Harold Knight and David Hale.

David was a farmer, Harold was a barber, and both lived in the Cadiz, Kentucky, area.

In the 1970s David wanted to kill a turkey, and he heard about this barber who, if you'd go to his barber shop, would make you a turkey call out of plastic prescription bottles and latex. What happened after that truly changed the hunting industry forever. Knight & Hale became the hunting equivalent of Proctor & Gamble in terms of a powerhouse of game call products.

For me, however, the grandeur of Knight & Hale wasn't in their legendary turkey calls. It was in the dispensation of their knowledge.

David and Harold hosted a television show called *Ultimate Hunting*. Yet even before that, they produced all sorts of magazines, cassette tapes, and eventually VHS tapes, not merely on how to kill a turkey, but also on how to grow as a turkey hunter. It was literally hunter discipleship.

I could write page after page on what I learned from those two giants during that time of my life. I bought every tape they had, listened to anything they said, and took it to heart.

What I valued most from David and Harold was how they helped me get into the mind of a gobbler.

If you're not a hunter, you're probably questioning my sanity on many levels about now. So pick your own poison to ponder what I'm saying here. . . .

If you're into investments, think about meeting a guru like J. Mark Mobius on Wall Street and talking about emerging markets. If you're a golfer, think about how giddy you were the first time you read Greg Norman's book *Shark Attack!,* in which he exposed his pathway to playing great golf.

Now imagine you grew up in the '80s and you actually got to play golf with Greg Norman. That very out-of-body experience happened to me when I got to hunt with David Hale for the first time.

That's me with David Hale on our first hunt together. To this day I can remember walking through a cut cornfield on one of his properties, and all I could think was, *I sure am glad it isn't daylight so that he can't see my face, because if he knew that all I can do is stare at him in disbelief that I'm actually hunting with him, he's going to think I'm a stalker.*

While I gained layers of knowledge from Knight & Hale, I can remember to this day when David told me, "If you'll listen to a tom, he'll tell you what he wants. Most hunters never pick up on that, Jason."

He told me, "If you yelp to a tom and nothing happens, and then you cluck a few times with a yelp, and he hammers back, keep doing that. So many guys will, let's say, cluck at him with no response, and the first time they yelp at him on a box call and he gobbles, they go right back to clucking on a slate call. Well, he just told you by his gobble that it was the sound of that hen yelp on a box call that stroked his ego...so stay with that."

The secret to killing a tom, or at least putting yourself in a better position to kill him, is simply to give him exactly what he wants. Right up until the moment you shoot him in the head.

OF TOMS AND DEVILS

What I've learned about the enemy is that more often than not, he doesn't come at you with what you don't want. He comes at you just as David taught me to go after a tom: by giving you everything you want.

The devil will have others tell you what you want to hear. He will put you in positions that fill your heart's desire when your motives are tainted but hard to discern. All along in that process, you are being set up.

Remember my buddy Brian Hinkle?

I asked him, "Where did all this start going bad?" His answer was immediate: "Five years ago. About five years ago I wanted to be the man, so I started buying really expensive bourbon and collecting it. Ultimately I began to let people into my life who had no business being in my circle."

For Brian it was the stroke of the ego.

I've found it's different for every man. The key is knowing that your enemy *is* in pursuit.

Never forget: the thief *comes.*

Never forget: the thief comes.

5 : BRUTAL FACT #5
IT'S CRITICAL TO KNOW WHY
YOU ARE A WANTED MAN

*Before you read any further, watch "Brutal Fact #5:
It's Critical to Know Why You Are a Wanted Man" at
JasonCruise.com/WantedMan.*

They called him the Working Man's Poet.

Merle Haggard sang real country music—the kind I wish would come back to Nashville, but that's for an entirely different book altogether, I suppose.

Hag's famous song "Branded Man" tells the story of a former prisoner turned legit. Yet no matter where he went, he had a number attached to his name. No matter what this man did, his identity was "branded."

I can think of nothing more accurate to describe who you are in the eyes of this "thief" Jesus talked about in John 10:10.

If you are "in Christ," then you are a branded man. Branded by the enemy as someone worth pursuing.

Have you ever stopped to consider why?

Is it because the devil is evil? Sure.

Is it because the devil enjoys inflicting harm? Sure it is, but that's not all.

> *If you are "in Christ," then you are a branded man.*

There's more to it than his evil nature being the driving force.

I don't think most Christ-following men have taken the time to think through their branded nature. I know I didn't for a long time.

The issue comes down to motive.

What would cause this enemy of yours to want you so badly? What would cause him to possess such an obsession with ushering into your life those things that steal, kill, and destroy?

While I am sure many reasons exist, the following come to mind immediately.

YOU BEAR THE IMAGE

Consider what is true about you now as opposed to what was true about you then—with "then" being the time before the Spirit of Christ inhabited your very being.

The scriptures have a lot to say about you, both then and now:

> *And you were dead in your trespasses and sins,*
> *in which you formerly walked according to the*
> *course of this world, according to the prince*
> *of the power of the air, of the spirit that is now*
> *working in the sons of disobedience. Among*
> *them we too all formerly lived in the lusts of*
> *our flesh, indulging the desires of the flesh and*
> *of the mind, and were by nature children of*
> *wrath, even as the rest. But God, being rich in*
> *mercy, because of His great love with which*
> *He loved us, even when we were dead in our*
> *transgressions, made us alive together with*

*Christ (by grace you have been saved), and
raised us up with Him, and seated us with Him
in the heavenly places in Christ Jesus, so that in
the ages to come He might show
the surpassing riches of His grace in
kindness toward us in Christ Jesus.*
EPHESIANS 2:1–7

Here Paul is talking about the "sons of disobedience," the tribe that once held your membership. Look at how the scriptures, the very breath of God, describe you.

Old Life: Dead. Trespasser. Sinner. Child of wrath.

New Life: Made alive. Saved. Seated with God. Object of rich grace.

Another one to ponder:

*We all, with unveiled face, beholding as
in a mirror the glory of the Lord, are being
transformed into the same image from glory to
glory, just as from the Lord, the Spirit.*
2 CORINTHIANS 3:18

Because Christ has ransomed the bodies, souls, and spirits of believers, we are the recipients of His glory, both now and in the life to come.

The devil cannot have that. He bears the image of evil. He has no redemption, nor will he ever.

He's much like a prisoner who only looks to do harm, for harm is all he has to offer. There is no hope left for him, and he knows it.

And one more:

> *Now in Christ Jesus you who formerly*
> *were far off have been brought near*
> *by the blood of Christ.*
> EPHESIANS 2:13

The believer is brought near, while the enemy was banished and pushed outside God's favor forever. He has no access to the King, but you do.

I could go on and on about this image-bearing idea, for the New Testament is saturated with the understanding that the Christ follower has been born again in the image of Christ.

Hundreds of adjectives describe how God sees you, and every time the enemy looks at a believer in Christ, he is reminded of everything he can never, ever be.

You bear the <u>image of Christ</u>, and being an image-bearer means you are a branded man. And that's why <u>Satan hates you so much</u>.

Study this concept and see how the devil is described throughout the New Testament. You will find that Jesus knew exactly who Satan is and the nature of this enemy we face.

You are everything Satan can never be, and for that reason alone you are hated. And hunted.

> *You are everything Satan can never be, and for that reason alone you are hated. And hunted.*

YOU ARE THE LINK TO OTHER PEOPLE HE CAN HARM

I genuinely believe the simple truth that you are the link to other people Satan can harm cannot be overstated. Even still, I have found it is something that none of us seems to consider in the heat of the moment.

The devil is a master networker. He is not just after you; he's after anything or anybody he can get to through you. Your life is a conduit of opportunity if he can infiltrate your daily grind.

Let's think about that saga from King David's life when he committed adultery with Bathsheba and then ordered the death of her husband (see 2 Samuel 11–12).

David's personal life wasn't the only thing affected by his sin. From one short-term affair came a domino effect of tragedy: David had Uriah killed. The child born from the affair between David and Bathsheba died. A kingdom and a nation were left to watch the outcome.

Read between the lines and see what you can see.

David had buddies—men he drank coffee with or hunted with at times. He had employees who were close to his heart. What about those guys? How were they affected by all that their spiritual leader had done? Imagine how incredibly hurt they must have felt over this affair.

Then there was Bathsheba. She also immediately felt the damage. Being David's mistress didn't change the fact that she still had to go to the market and buy groceries. Imagine the whispers, the stares.

The domino effect of sin reaches amazingly far and can deeply touch the lives of people who are not even involved.

I suppose none of us would ever sin if the consequences were immediate and obvious. <u>The nature of sin is, at first, to stay hidden,</u> but you can be sure that all of your clandestine excursions off the path of Christ will eventually go public.

> *The domino effect of sin reaches amazingly far and can deeply touch the lives of people who are not even involved.*

CONSIDERING THE COST

Jesus talked often about being a disciple. He was trying to get His listeners to understand just how critical it is that a man knows what he's doing if he decides to follow the Nazarene. He asked, "For which one of you, when he wants to build a tower, does not first sit down and calculate the cost to see if he has enough to complete it?" (Luke 14:28).

This one simple practice has helped me many times: when faced with any decision, I ask myself, *Is this a short-term gain*

CRITICAL TO KNOW WHY YOU ARE A WANTED MAN

for a long-term loss?

I cannot tell you how many times that single question has revealed an impure motive residing in my heart.

Sin has a catastrophic footprint that imprints people anywhere near the tread point. Being in ministry since the 1990s, I can tell you that I've had a front-row seat to watching the effects sin has on the lives of people who were just on the periphery.

I know a guy who just a few months ago was sentenced to several years of prison for white-collar financial crimes. Hundreds of unsuspecting employees lost their careers and were left without a paycheck because of his endeavors. Their wives, their husbands, their children, their parents—all were hurt because of one man's disobedience.

> *The bigger picture is immediately brought into view when you consider the cost, and, my brother, costs must be considered, for the stakes of the game are so very high.*

You have your own stories, too. Some of those stories

BRUTAL FACT #5

you've lived out personally. You have the scars to prove it.

Keep the idea of longevity in front of you as you trek through life outside the wire. It will force you to maintain clarity in a foggy land.

Short term versus long term is a sobering concept. The bigger picture is immediately brought into view when you consider the cost, and, my brother, costs must be considered, for the stakes of the game are so very high.

A LYRIC TO CONSIDER

God has given me several men in my life who have proven to be true sages. They are men of righteous intent who keep me moving forward in my walk with Christ. One of those men is Steve Chapman. He's half of the musical duo of Steve and Annie Chapman. Steve is a singer-songwriter who has also written several books. He's also a hunter, and we hunt together often.

Like many of those musical freaks of nature walking around the greater Nashville area, he has an amazing knack for turning common phrases into lyrics.

102
JASON CRUISE

Many years ago we were on a turkey hunt and we began to talk about marriage. He started telling me of a song he was writing about the cost of what appear to be short-term gains but are truly long-term losses.

He said, "I've got this phrase about what I wouldn't give for a chance to stray just a little from Annie." The first few lines of the song are:

> *She gave that signal, she had that walk.*
> *Something inside me began to talk.*
> *Said, "Ain't she fine?" I said, "I agree."*
> *I felt the danger when she looked at me.*
>
> *I started thinkin' how she would feel;*
> *I started wonderin' how I might close the deal.*
> *I could say I didn't when I really did.*
> *If I could have her, what I wouldn't give.*
> *Ooh, what I wouldn't give.*
>
> *My wife. Her smile. Our memories. The miles.*
> *Our children. Their trust.*
> *And everything that God has given us.*
> *That's what I wouldn't give for her.*[1]

And in the same vein:

> *Do not give your strength to women,*
> *Or your ways to that which destroys kings.*
> PROVERBS 31:3

We all the know that the reality of life outside the wire is that casualties will happen. So when the time and season enters your life, what do you do next?

6 : SOMETHING UNEXPECTED

As I put pen to paper for this book, I began to realize that a chapter about navigating failure would be beyond question the most needed chapter of all—and for blatantly obvious reasons: every man fails.

Darren Tyler, a close friend of mine who is a recording artist manager turned preacher, often says it this way: "Friends, none of us are getting out of this thing unscathed."

It is a painful, sober reality of which Darren speaks.

No man will leave this earth and exchange this world for the next without scars, bruises, and his own fair share of deep wounds from sins committed and sins received, along with a fair mixture of wounds that life gives to our friends and family. And some of those scars will remain fresh until the day we meet Jesus.

> *Every man fails.*

Right now, in preparation for scholastic-level football, my sons are playing flag football for the YMCA. I'm the coach. It's absolutely the coolest thing ever, because I have an opportunity to inject so many formative life lessons into their young souls. It's equally sobering for the same reason. I know I'll be accountable for these kids someday; therefore I do not take my responsibility lightly.

My older son, Cole, is more risk averse than my younger son, Tucker. Cole is a planner. He's like his mama. He is what she and I often refer to as a "sizer-upper." He doesn't just jump into the pool because all the other kids are swimming. No, he's going to take a few minutes, look at the water, evaluate the risk level, and then make a decision.

Tucker is a different story altogether. He's liable to jump in the water without taking the time to put on his swim trunks. With Tucker, there are no questions and no measurements—just possibilities. Endless possibilities and adventures to be had.

Though he's young now, Cole is a super-skilled quarterback. Who knows if he'll carry that through to junior high or high school, but for now he's really excelling at that position.

I felt weird putting him at QB in the early years (we started playing when he was six years old). You know, because I'm the coach and my kid is playing QB. . .all that jazz. The problem, however, was simple: when you have a bunch of knot-headed six-year-olds, somebody has to know what's going on at the line of scrimmage.

I asked an older coach who had coached his sons until they moved up to a junior high team, "What were your biggest challenges when they were age six?"

Without hesitation he said, "You must, without question, get the snap off, which means that if you don't have two kids—a quarterback and a center—who can make the exchange, know their roles, know the playbook well, and have good hand-eye coordination. . ." I can still hear him saying, "If you don't get that part right, it's all going to fall apart before the play even develops."

Cole, since he could barely walk, has had amazing hand-eye coordination. So, not knowing any of the other kids, I began to run him at center and also QB, because Cole is dependable. Crazy dependable. He's coachable, and with that age group I needed "coachable" in a bad, bad way.

Cole is not a racehorse. At least not yet. He's a pack mule. Steady. Reliable. Strategic.

However, Cole has a great arm to go along with his strategic self. He's crazy accurate. So he's coming along great as a quarterback.

The problem is, like most people who are strategic planners, Cole tends to be risk averse. He is easily devastated by failures of the smallest kind. His greatest nightmare is that he has let you down.

No, he doesn't shed tears at a poorly thrown ball, nor does he freak out if he misses a shot at a gobbler on a turkey hunt; but you can bet the farm on the fact that his mistakes do not exit his mind easily. He'll dwell on them if you let him. He'll get down on himself if he's not careful.

This leads me to my point about every man, Cole included.

I've told Cole time and time again, "Son, show me any champion in sports or in business, and I'll show you a man whose past is riddled with failures. The difference between him and a guy you've never heard of is that a champion refused to be defined by his failures."

I tell Cole over and over again that the difference between champions and the rest of the world is that champions move past their failures and move on to possibilities that only exist—that only live—in the future.

The more I've thought about living life outside the wire, the more Darren Tyler's words haunt me.

We are, in fact, not escaping this journey unscathed. We all are going to be wounded by our enemy.

That is perhaps the most brutal fact of them all.

Hollywood it may be, but Rocky Balboa said it well:

> Let me tell you something you already know. The world ain't all sunshine and rainbows. It's a very mean and nasty place, and I don't care how tough you are, it will beat you to your knees and keep you there permanently if you let it. You, me, or nobody is gonna hit as hard as life. But it ain't about how hard you hit. It's about how hard you can get hit and keep moving forward; how much you can take and keep moving forward. That's how winning is done!

You are going to get hit. You live outside the wire. Daily. You are going to get hit, and when you do, you're going to need some truths underneath you during that season of contingency-gone-into-action.

A WANTED MAN   109

> *You are going to get hit, and when you do, you're going to need some truths underneath you during that season of contingency-gone-into-action.*

From here I'm going to share some insights with you that I've gained over the years. Some I've learned from navigating my own failures, and some I've learned by watching other men pull out of times and seasons when they were wounded by the thief.

7 : BRUTAL FACT #6 YOU MUST NAVIGATE FAILURE *AND* DO IT WITH BRUTAL HOPE

Before you read any further, watch "Brutal Fact #6: Navigating Failure" at JasonCruise.com/WantedMan.

You will fail.

This fact is all too familiar because you've lived it.

I've always been fascinated with business and the marketplace. God did not call me to further His kingdom through business, but I believe with all my heart that the marketplace is where God and His work in people's lives are most overlooked.

Think about it: Christians go to church once a week, but life happens at work. If you don't believe that, then just start messing with someone's career path and watch what happens next! Depression, panic, stress on the marriage, and other anxieties come from what happens to a person in the marketplace.

Marketplace cultures are great educators of human nature, and one such prophet to that world, professor, consultant, and author Jim Collins, has provided vast wisdom as to how people move, breathe, and operate in successful companies.

As I mentioned previously, Collins wrote one of the greatest business books of all time, *Good to Great*. It is an amazing book—not about how to run a business, but about how great leaders in business think. He also pioneered new ground with his work *How the Mighty Fall*. It's a study on how great companies—ones with such legendary names as Hewlett-Packard, Motorola, Zenith, and so on—fell in epic proportions from being icons of business to utter failures or at least shadows of their former selves.

In his research of failed business cultures, Collins made a simple, brutal observation about failure:

> *Every institution is vulnerable, no matter how great. No matter how much you've achieved, no matter how far you've gone, no matter how much power you've garnered, you are vulnerable to*

<u>decline</u>. *There is no law of nature that the most powerful will inevitably remain at the top. <u>Anyone can fail and most eventually do</u>.*[1]

Are Collins's findings anything new when contrasted with scripture? *No.*

Is not human failure at the center of the biblical story? Of course it is.

That's what I love about the heart of God in terms of how He chose to tell His story—our story. <u>God never covers over human failure; for in failure, we see the possibility of rising again—but only through divine intervention in one man: Christ alone</u>.

Over and over again we see failure in scripture. In fact, you could say scripture is one failure story after another, with short interludes in which somebody occasionally gets it right.

The thing is, we are misled about Bible characters from the youngest age.

Now before you go thinking I'm blaming your Sunday school teachers for being deceptive, I am not. No, what I am saying is that we often don't know what to do with the very ugly side of humanity found in these Bible characters we idolize.

Moses is often seen as a *giant* of a man with a deep voice

who commanded Pharaoh to release God's people. Did Moses do that? Yes, he certainly did. The deep voice? Maybe that's just a Hollywood effect.

<u>Moses straight up killed a dude</u>, too.

With his bare hands, Moses beat a guy to death. Then he lived the life of a homeless vagabond. Not the sort of beacon of hope we want to show our kids when they are searching for a career path.

<u>Noah was a kingpin of reckless faith</u>. He was a guy everybody thought to be the village idiot—right up until the day it started raining. Think about it: Noah had never seen rain before because God irrigated the earth from the ground up in those days. So did Noah have the kind of unquestioning faith that compelled him to build a boat for a catastrophic event for which he had no mental frame of reference? Yep, he sure did. <u>That sort of faith was so abnormal we'd call it "faith of biblical proportions."</u>

Not long after that event, this same Noah got so drunk that he took off all his clothes and passed out. As we'd say in the South, "He got *nekid*."

Noah lost his ever-loving mind for a moment and embarrassed his entire family.

So, yeah, I could go on and on about how many people in scripture failed in epic proportions. Failed their families.

Failed their colleagues. Failed the church. Failed God.

Failure, or at least navigating it, is the story of our lives in many ways. However, we don't talk about the seemingly negative aspects of biblical characters' lives until students reach the high school youth group—if at all! So if there's one brutal truth we must embrace, it's that failure, in many ways, is inevitable in all of our lives.

Jim Collins is right: "Anyone can fail and most eventually do."

You know what it means to lose money from poor decisions with credit cards. You know what it means to look into your wife's eyes and try to explain why looking at porn has nothing to do with how you look at her. You know what it feels like to let people down, and you know what it feels like to be let down. Every man everywhere fails.

The mountain to climb, then, becomes not one of how to avoid mistakes, but more so how to recover from mistakes made.

> *God can take something ugly and mend it to a state where it can be used again.*

✓ Victory is what brings beauty to the failure.

✓ Victory is what makes failure worth enduring.

✓ Victory is what makes hope something more than a fantasy. And that, too, my brother, is the story of scripture: that God can reconcile all of your failures in Christ. He can take something ugly and mend it to a state where it can be used again.

OWN THE FAILURE

I have been in full-time ministry since 1990. Yes, I started early. Way early. However, that gave me one distinct advantage: I've had a front-row seat to see how real people's mistakes with money, marriage, relationships, and leadership have destroyed the heartbeat of life. I've seen far too many times how failure, once it has gone septic, wrecks the entire ecosystem of a man's world.

Perhaps the single most common trait I see in men when something gets broke is that most deflect responsibility. They admit a mistake but then transfer blame, or they might take 70 percent of the failure while the other 30 percent "is not my fault."

No, you chose to do it, so own it.

No more lies.

When you fail, you have to make a renegade commitment to stop all the lies. Lies and deception are what got you in a bad place.

The enemy lies to us all. In fact, that's where all sin begins. So you have to own it to get out of its path.

I'm not into quoting long passages of scripture, but this time it's different. You must read all fourteen verses of the passage that follows to see the context or it won't necessarily make sense. After you have read the passage, we'll break it down man to man.

> *The enemy lies to us all. In fact, that's where all sin begins. So you have to own it to get out of its path.*

We've already glanced at this sad soap opera earlier, but here's the backstory: David, Israel's king at the time, has an affair with a woman named Bathsheba, who was married to Uriah, one of David's chief battle officers.

David and Bathsheba do the deed, and she gets

pregnant. Stress causes panic. <u>Stress causes a man to take short-term gains for long-term losses,</u> because stress clouds <u>perspective.</u>

So in a season of stress and panic, David has an idea. Israel is in the middle of a war, so David sends Uriah straight to the front lines in hopes that he'll get killed in battle, die a hero's death, and no one will be any the wiser that this new baby who comes along is not Uriah's.

God does intervene, but not until after Uriah dies in battle.

Nathan, a prophet, does something that most people overlook: he risks his life to tell the truth.

Churchgoing people read this story as if Nathan just strolls into the king's main office and calls out David on the spot for what he's done. Listen, do you really think it was that easy? Nathan knew that all David had to do was motion to his guards and say, "Kill him, bury the body, and do it quietly."

This was not the Internet age when every human being walking the planet is only a smartphone video away from being a live-on-the-scene reporter.

You could bury people much easier back then.

Think about it: David had just had Uriah killed, so what's two dead bodies? Don't you think Nathan knew that?

Nathan risked his life to tell David the truth on God's behalf.

This is how that conversation played out:

*Then the LORD sent Nathan to David. And he came
to him and said, "There were two men in one city,
the one rich and the other poor. The rich man had
a great many flocks and herds. But the poor man
had nothing except one little ewe lamb which he
bought and nourished; and it grew up together
with him and his children. It would eat of his bread
and drink of his cup and lie in his bosom, and was
like a daughter to him. Now a traveler came to
the rich man, and he was unwilling to take from
his own flock or his own herd, to prepare for the
wayfarer who had come to him; rather he took the
poor man's ewe lamb and prepared it for the man
who had come to him."*

*Then David's anger burned greatly against
the man, and he said to Nathan, "As the LORD
lives, surely the man who has done this deserves
to die. He must make restitution for the lamb
fourfold, because he did this thing and had no
compassion."*

*Nathan then said to David, "You are the
man! Thus says the LORD God of Israel, 'It is I*

who anointed you king over Israel and it is I who delivered you from the hand of Saul. I also gave you your master's house and your master's wives into your care, and I gave you the house of Israel and Judah; and if that had been too little, I would have added to you many more things like these! Why have you despised the word of the LORD by doing evil in His sight? You have struck down Uriah the Hittite with the sword, have taken his wife to be your wife, and have killed him with the sword of the sons of Ammon. Now therefore, the sword shall never depart from your house, because you have despised Me and have taken the wife of Uriah the Hittite to be your wife.' Thus says the LORD, 'Behold, I will raise up evil against you from your own household; I will even take your wives before your eyes and give them to your companion, and he will lie with your wives in broad daylight. Indeed you did it secretly, but I will do this thing before all Israel, and under the sun.'"

Then David said to Nathan, "I have sinned against the LORD." And Nathan said to David, "The LORD also has taken away your sin; you shall not die. However, because by this deed you have given occasion to the enemies of the LORD to blaspheme, the child also that is born to you shall surely die."

2 SAMUEL 12:1–14

The interesting aspect of this story to me is that <u>David owned the sin</u>. <u>And because he owned the sin,</u> the lies stopped. The <u>self-deception</u> stopped. The confusion stopped.

What do you want to bet that, on that very day, David's vision became clearer? I can almost guarantee you that he gained clarity right then and there.

✓ Did the pain vanish? No, not at all.

✓ Did the rumors stop dead in their tracks? No.

✓ Did David all of a sudden know exactly what to do next? Probably not.

The consequences still felt staggering, but the lies did stop that day. When lies stop, healing is at least a possibility.

Imagine how much worse this situation would have become, how many more people would have been hurt—or killed—had this king, who held absolute power and authority over his people, kept on inventing cover-ups for the other cover-ups.

Think about it.

Did it ever occur to you that sin, every single brand of sin in existence, has one common denominator? Each one starts with the sinner believing some form of lie.

For David to sin against God, he had to accept some form of lie. Maybe the lie was "Who's ever going to know about it?" or "You're the king; do what you want." And on and on it goes.

Lies are the starting point for sin, and if you want to stop the lies, you have to own the failure first.

> *There is no other first step back to righteousness. Owning the failure is the first and only way to freedom.*

When you refuse to fully own the failure, you only prolong the healing process. Deflecting responsibility causes more damage because the people closest to you pull themselves further and further away because of your arrogance in refusing to accept what has happened.

Own the failure. Own it.

There is no other first step back to righteousness. Owning the failure is the first and only way to freedom.

BRING EVERYTHING INTO THE LIGHT

Lies, deceit, and wrongdoings are what get a man into moral and spiritual failure, so a man must be committed to walking every next step after the failure in the light of Christ.

Surgery is always done in the light; it is never done in the dark.

Darkness is where infection dwells. What's the first thing you do when you start to fix something, operate on something, or repair something? Get some light on it so you can see clearly. Surgeons, mechanics, electricians, computer repair gurus, home contractors, HVAC mechanics, and plumbers all have something in common: they shine a light right onto the problem when they are making assessments.

So why, then, does a man—when he's failed his family, his friends, his boss, or just himself—want to conceal his failure?

Normally it's a toxic concoction of embarrassment and fear mixed with a small dose of leftover pride.

"THE DEVIL FINALLY GOT ME"

"The devil finally got me." That's what my friend said to me many years ago on the worst day of his life. We were sitting in his kitchen talking about a plan to move him forward in life. I don't know why, but I remember it as clear as if it happened just last week.

Late the night before, his wife had called me. When I answered the phone, she was sobbing hysterically. I felt fully convinced that someone, perhaps her husband, had been killed in a car wreck and I was her first call. It was that sort of loud, screaming panic on the phone.

She couldn't express anything of substance but wailing.

She kept saying my name over and over again through weeping and tears. "Jason, oh no, Jason. Jason, help me. Oh no, oh no!"

It took me five minutes to get her to a place where she wasn't completely hysterical with panic.

"What happened? Take a deep breath and just tell me what happened."

Finally, in a weak voice, she said, "I noticed we were getting some strange bills, and I looked into it and something looked way out of place. I asked him about it, and he just started crying."

She then shared, "He just told me that we are deep in debt. Way, way in debt, and I had no idea about it whatsoever. I'm afraid we are going to lose everything we've got."

What her husband had done, was what happened to so many people. It's an old play in a toxic playbook. Once the financial trouble started, he started to use one credit card to pay off another.

So there we were, standing in his kitchen, and he said, "The devil finally got me, Jason. That's all I can say."

My response totally shocked him.

I mean, honestly, it shocked him to the core.

I said to him, "No, my brother, the devil didn't do this to you. No, in fact, God just did you the biggest favor you ever could have asked since all this started."

He just looked at me, so I went on. "Yes, you let the devil influence you, and you got yourself into this awful mess with his demonic influence, but today God brought all the walls down. Today God showed His love for you by taking away every way you could continue the lies and deceit. God has stripped away every cover and brought the lies into the light where you're forced to deal with them."

He sat there in silence.

I continued to explain to my friend that God's discipline is His love. I walked him through how God had intervened.

He'd been praying for God to get him out of his mess. And so God did just that, but God wasn't going to get him out of it through the continued employment of lies.

Why? Because the love of God doesn't live in the dark. God's sovereign grace doesn't operate in shadow games and deception.

No. <u>God deals only in the light</u>.

Let's go back to the verse that started the idea that eventually became this book: "The thief comes only to steal and kill and destroy" (John 10:10).

God deals only in the light.

When you bring all the facts into the light, you leave no more room for your enemy to steal, kill, or destroy.

Why does a mechanic shine multiple sets of lights onto an engine when he's working on it? Because the light gives him different angles to see things previously hidden.

Every great mechanic I know wants a few lights on

a problem to show all the issues he's dealing with at the moment.

My friend had accumulated thousands upon tens of thousands of dollars of debt, and he finally came to the place where lies weren't able to cover him anymore. It was then that he and his wife developed a plan to recover from it together, which included bankruptcy.

Life was really tough for them financially during those next few, cold years, but they made it. They made it together.

Can you imagine what life would be like today had the lies and cover-ups continued? There's no telling how much hidden debt he'd have acquired just trying to keep his wife from knowing about it.

HEADLAMPS

I duck hunt. And I love it. Duck hunting done well is a ton of work. There's so much gear involved that it's often pure labor, but when you love something, it doesn't feel so much like work.

There is one piece of gear that makes life much easier for a duck hunter: the headlamp.

If you don't have a headlamp, life can get painful—or painfully wet—for you on a duck hunt.

Your word is a lamp to my feet and a light to my path.
PSALM 119:105

Think about that. A lamp to my feet. A light to my path.

In other words, this kind of light is not a spotlight. Not a QBeam that casts a ray of sunshine in the darkness for three hundred yards, but just enough light to keep you steady and upright for the next few steps.

I think, at least for me, the hardest part of failure is forcing myself to bring my failure into the light.

Light is painful at first. It shows you all the flawed and

broken areas. Those areas are ugly and embarrassing. You find yourself asking, "How in the world did I not see that? It seems so obvious."

The reason: darkness hides things.

The enemy blinds you with darkness when you allow him— which is why light matters more than ever when you fail. Light is critical to your recovery. So bring all your sin into the light.

Once the bomb of failure has exploded, you're already embarrassed and broken. Use that to your advantage and get everything in the light.

> *Once the bomb of failure has exploded, you're already embarrassed and broken. Use that to your advantage and get everything in the light.*

IN A DIFFERENT LIGHT

This idea of living in the light begs a different question: Why do so many men refuse to allow full, unfiltered light onto a sin situation?

In a word: _arrogance._

People often refer to pride as the reason for a person's downfall. I've discovered, however, that in many cases it wasn't pride, but arrogance, that caused a person to fall into ruin.

Arrogance is the ability to deceive yourself into believing a lie. I've seen far too many men take on the attitude, "Yes, the enemy is real, but I'm not going to succumb to cashing in all I know to be true to chase a fantasy."

Several years ago I studied the book of Proverbs. I wouldn't say it was a deep study of this wisdom book; I simply began to work through the thirty-one chapters looking for the overtones of the individual chapters themselves.

I wasn't prepared for one small takeaway. It was a discovery that simply reinforced what I had learned many times from studying scripture: arrogance is paramount in most every man's life.

Almost every single chapter of Proverbs has at least one verse warning about the dangers of arrogance.

In fact, entire chapters in the book of Proverbs are devoted to warning a man about how fast his ruin will come if he takes on an arrogant spirit.

Arrogance shows up when a man fails and then refuses to bring the failure into unfiltered light. Arrogance shows

{ up when a man fails and refuses to accept full responsibility. } Arrogance clouds perspective, and, my brother, perspective is what you need when you fail.

REALIZE THAT NO CHAMPION IS WITHOUT A COACH

Look, if you woke up tonight with a severe toothache shearing through your jawbone, you wouldn't think twice about calling a dentist immediately the next morning.

Yet the vast majority of men who experience the pain and obstacles caused by failure won't get professional counseling. Pride and arrogance are what got them into a predicament in the first place, and now pride and arrogance are keeping them from getting help.

Many men think that if they can just "do better" and clean up their lives, their bad situation will go away.

Brother, let me save you some unnecessary heartache: your situation won't self-correct. Hard work may help solve the problem, but there is collateral damage when you fail, and you know it.

Kids are involved. Employers often get dragged into the

BRUTAL FACT #6

drama. Wives feel the huge brunt of our sins, whatever they may be.

You need a Spirit-filled professional, who knows the Word of God well, to hitch up with you and walk you through the wilderness.

A wilderness is what you have coming for a year or more in front of you. When the bomb goes off and your failures come calling, you don't just repent and then everything gets better.

Jesus forgives, but the scars take time to heal. And you're going to need help to make that healing process progress to completion.

> *Jesus forgives, but the scars take time to heal.*

AN AMERICAN ICON ON SEEKING WISDOM

A fascinating story that sheds light on an American business icon further drives home why this one man is such a legend, even though he passed on many years ago. After reading Jim Collins's account of the story, *How the Mighty Fall*, I did some research, but it was hard to find more depth on the topic. Gleaning from Collins's account of it, it is truly fascinating to me.

The story, says Collins, has its roots in the retail chain store brand Ames Department Stores.

In the 1970s and '80s, Ames had solid success. Some researchers even say their stock in many ways rivaled that of Walmart.

In the late 1980s, a handful of Brazilian investors purchased the Ames brand. Wanting to gain a more solid understanding of their market share, they sought out meetings with American business owners who were winning in the retail marketplace.

Now, you have to realize that we are so comfortable today with the free and easy access to information that we tend to forget just how difficult this next chapter of the story would be for those leading a business in that era.

They had no Google, no LinkedIn, no online way to find a corporate phone number with the scroll of a thumb across a smartphone screen, no easy way to reach straight through the red-tape tangle and talk with these business leaders one-on-one.

These were the days still deeply mired in landlines, phone books, and snail mail. You know—the days when you had to go to the library to find information, as I mentioned earlier.

So these Brazilian marketplace capitalists did the only thing a person could do if he wasn't networked with someone on the inside of a corporation: they wrote letters!

They sent letters to many high-level CEOs who led companies in the American retail marketplace, asking if they themselves could come to America, meet with these leaders, and learn from their wisdom about running department stores.

Here's a shocker: not a single CEO responded.

Except one.

Upon receiving word that this CEO would meet with them, the Brazilian businessmen boarded a plane. Upon touching down, they were stunned at the man standing before them in the small regional airport.

He had no driver, no red carpet, no corporate liaison team

of attorneys to vet these Brazilian wisdom seekers. No, he just showed up at the airport in a pickup truck—accompanied by his dog, Ol' Roy—to pick up his guests.

His name was Sam Walton.

Now just for a second, can't you picture this in your mind? It wasn't like Sam Walton was still a no-name. Walmart was well established and on the scene in the 1980s and was getting huge reviews in the media world of the corporate sector.

There stands Sam Walton.

I picture him wearing an old pair of khaki pants, a button-down shirt, and a humble grin as the Brazilians approach.

Having been to Arkansas many times to duck hunt, I can hear him now: "Hey, boys. Glad y'all could come see me. It's nice to meet you."

He takes them out of Northwest Arkansas Regional Airport, and there in the back of his truck sits his dog.

It's like a scene out of an *Andy Griffith Show* episode.

As the story goes, Walton actually took the businessmen to his home and they sat in his kitchen.[2]

The strange and unexpected turn in the story is that the Brazilian investors couldn't get over how many questions Walton actually had for them. He quizzed them about their data, thought through their insights on retail, and pushed to learn from them. He was more than intrigued by their venture. From the reports of how this trip played out, Walton wanted to gain their wisdom and insight from the research they'd executed in the due diligence phase of buying the Ames brand.

The Brazilians, however, were no doubt thinking, *This is Sam Walton. He's already crazy successful.*

I get it. I would be stunned, too, at why this rising corporate legend would be so intrigued to know what I thought about the marketplace.

Sam Walton seemingly had a pure and sincere willingness to get counsel. He valued being a lifelong learner.

Walton wasn't too smart to be educated, even in a field of knowledge where he was considered a top-level expert.

When it comes to success, whether that is spiritual success, financial success, marital success, or going from a 12 handicap to a 4, my experience is that the common denominator among successful people is that they value learning.

Think about it: you've just gone through an epic failure. Something went way, way wrong. It isn't that you're not intelligent. No, it's not at all about "smarts." It is about humility. It is about asking questions of people who love you enough to tell you the truth. It is about being willing to reassess your trajectory.

And it's about desiring to do what wisdom demands, even when doing so is difficult or inconvenient.

What is the point of seeking counsel if you don't follow through with what you are being told about recovery?

> *What is the point of seeking counsel if you don't follow through with what you are being told about recovery?*

BE WILLING TO SEPARATE YOURSELF

I'll never forget the conversation. It wasn't rocket science; in fact, what my friend Greg was telling me about life after giving up on dealing drugs sounded like commonsense stuff.

Greg grew up in a world far different from the home life I'd experienced. His was a Jekyll-and-Hyde type of world. His parents were divorced, so his family life had all sorts of dynamics with new siblings and new environments where instability was the norm. Greg split time between families and could pretty much do what he wanted when he wanted.

Money was scarce, so Greg ended up selling drugs and

sold them all the way into his senior year in high school.

One day during our sophomore year in college, we were sitting on the tennis court talking, and somehow we got on the topic of our formative years in high school.

Greg had come to Christ during his senior year and had a testimony that was having an impact on people all throughout his community. Eventually our conversation turned to our career paths. We were both working simple retail jobs at the time.

Greg said, "You know, Cruise, I'm making minimum wage—$3.25 an hour in an honest job at the age of twenty. I'm making about $28 a day now, and I was making about $100 in five minutes when I was fifteen, selling drugs. I'd make a thousand dollars a week and work just a few hours at the most."

We laughed at the irony. He had no desire to go back there, but the contrast was mind-bending for him.

It was then that I asked him, "Greg, what did it take for you to finally get off of drugs and out of that world?"

He said, "You know, Jason, I know this sounds like something you'd hear in a high school public service announcement, but honestly nothing changed with me and drugs until I stopped running with the people who did drugs. Nothing changed until I changed those closest to me."

FRIENDS VS. BROTHERS

Being in ministry for more than twenty years has shown me a lot about people. For whatever reason, compared to most ministers I know, I've had more than the average minister's experience in dealing with people who are locked up in addiction.

The comical absurdity with addicts is that they honestly do fear leaving the lifestyle for many reasons, and one of those is that they think they'll <u>lose their friends</u>. They really believe their friends love them deeply, and they don't want to lose that network.

I've driven many people to inpatient rehabilitation facilities for a three-week stay to get clean, and do you know that 100 percent of the time, the friends of an addict have never even bothered to call and check on how the person was doing?

It's funny to see the look on the face of an addict when I ask, "Hey, have your friends given you any support or checked in on you to encourage you through the process?"

There's always a strange look of bewilderment as they say, "You know, not one. No one called or checked up on me."

IF IT WAS GOOD ENOUGH FOR JESUS: THE POWER OF SMALL GROUPS

You cannot be naive once failure has entered your life. And that includes being naive about whom you choose to let get closest to you.

I promise you I'm not being a shock jock when I say this. No drama intended, but I'm serious when I say that I don't believe that Christians as a whole, since the day Jesus ascended into heaven, have ever been able to understand or accept the critical need to have a small group of brothers protecting our blind spots.

Sure, most of us have had other men around us in life's normal flow on some level, but camaraderie is at the core of what Jesus did by placing Himself near a small group men.

Think about this: Jesus knew from the beginning of his ministry that His days were numbered. And I'm not talking about numbered in terms of moving out into a new career field.

No, Jesus knew that his retirement party was just a short time off and that it involved the most horrific murder in human history in the form of a torture device called a Roman cross.

Now think about this: If you knew that you were going to die in just a few years, or sooner, would you spend the remaining time you had left with just twelve people? Honestly, I'm not sure any American evangelical Christian really "gets" the gravity in Jesus' decision to take that route—myself certainly included.

Every man needs his own tribe. Men who know his habits, his tendencies, and his weaknesses, and yet know how to rely on his skill set to offset their own deficiencies.

There's power in a small group. We toss around this "band of brothers" idea in Christendom quite freely these days, but in truth that's what brotherhood really should be: men who fight for and alongside one another. Every man needs his own tribe. Men who know his habits, his tendencies, and his weaknesses, and yet know how to rely on his skill set to offset their own deficiencies.

Yes. That is the way biblical manhood should be. We owe

that to one another. The older I get, however, I'm finding that a band of brothers is rare. You can't find that kind of community easily, and if you do, you probably had to help invent it as part of the culture you run with on a daily basis.

Most men don't have the grit for the hard work that brotherhood done right takes. To be sustainable, true brotherhood requires, relational, life-on-life, intentional work, and due to that level of emotional maintenance, the vast majority of men mentally say, *Count me out*. It's just too much work for most men. We aren't wired for maintenance, and so because brotherhood involves emotional maintenance, we check out fast.

The problem is that Jesus told us in Matthew 28:19 to "make disciples." He never instructed us to make converts, but converts are mostly what we see today.

That's because making disciples is hard work. I am convinced that most men don't have the wherewithal to do it because it asks for too much transparency. Yet what's the alternative? If you cut yourself off from your brothers, you're going to hit the ditch—hard. It's only a matter of time. Then what do you get? You get all the mess that comes with it. So in terms of investment, you pay a high price for such temporary privacy. The return on investment is no return at all.

REALIZE THAT THIS RECENT FAILURE IS BUT ONE CHAPTER OF YOUR LIFE

Yes, your failure is a bad chapter of your life—a really, really bad chapter. But it's not the full story summing up your life.

Be very careful that you do not minimize the trauma you've caused. I've seen far too many men do that. We do it out of embarrassment, mainly. When you've let everyone down, and you know it, then it can be almost too much to accept.

Time after time I've seen men fall on their spiritual, and sometimes physical, faces, and while they know it isn't good, I'll hear them say things like, "Oh, I'll be all right. Just a bump in the road. Gotta keep moving."

> *Yes, your failure is a bad chapter of your life—a really, really bad chapter. But it's not the full story summing up your life.*

When you hear that coming from a man who has wrecked his career, his family, or both, you can bet the nightmare is not over. Accepting failure is something we are unable to avoid because failure has been a part of our story since the experience of Adam and Eve in the Garden of Eden.

Paul said in Romans 5:12, "Through one man sin entered into the world, and death through sin, and so death spread to all men, because all sinned." Adam took us down the road of sin. Yes, it's true. However, had you or I been there, we'd have done the same. Sin is a part of our nature, and there's no denying that simple reality.

I remember being in a class working on my master's degree during my seminary years. We were in Systematic Theology, which is a brutal class for both the student and the professor. Think about it: you're discussing the things of God, and that can get about as wild and dramatic as a classroom setting can get, no matter who is in the room.

One student asked our professor, "Are we <u>born sinners</u>, or do we become sinners?"

The professor was a great guy with a good heart. He had some soft views of God that made me question him at times, but he was a true believer. I felt sorry for him, because for many students, he just wasn't dogmatic enough, so they would forever try to corner him on a piece of theology that didn't fit the denominational creed. Time after time a few students would try to draw him out on a thin limb, hoping he'd snap it.

Even still, it was a good question. I'll admit that. It's a super question, really, because it reveals a lot—about a lot. If we are born sinners, God set us up for failure, some would argue. If we become sinners, then it's all on us.

I loved the way my professor answered it. He gently laughed and said, "It doesn't matter. It doesn't matter at all. Either way, you're going to sin. There's no escaping it. You're destined to sin for one simple reason: there's only one God, and you're not Him."

There was no rebuttal. None whatsoever.

It's a strange thing, sin.

Liberals and conservatives alike know they have it in their bones.

Sin is something you must accept as a reality. Remember that conversation you and I had earlier about owning failure? You must own it, and part of owning it is eventually coming to accept sin as something you cannot change.

The longer and the deeper I walk the path of Christ, the more I find that my own personal goodness, whatever it may be, is still wretched comedy.

And there is where you must start. It's at the crossroads of shame and sustainability that every man must make a conscious decision: Will I live in shame, or will I find a sustainable way to move forward?

I can think of few things worse than a man who gets kicked in the teeth by his failures and just sits there and bleeds over it for the next forty years.

I've seen men do it. It's an ugly, ugly thing.

WINNING MATTERS

Back to coaching my two sons in football.

Let me tell you one huge problem I have with our culture of parenting today. We live in a society where everybody gets a trophy for showing up and playing, and that's just stupid. In fact, it's more than stupid; it is immobilizing. All we are doing is setting kids up for the brutal truth that life doesn't throw you a trophy party just for getting out of bed every day.

While this soft, nurturing mentality so many parents buy into today is prevalent and tends to go over well with crowds of parents in the stands, I do not and will not subscribe to it.

Look, I've never been the kind of coach who has a win-at-all-costs mentality. I want my sons, and all my players, to learn how to lose with honor.

I have a mandatory coach-parent meeting every year at the first practice of the season. In that meeting I let parents know I will never, ever teach their sons to be good losers. Show me a good loser, and I'll show you someone who has never learned how to win nor tasted the sweet experience winning brings.

I always tell parents in that setting, "I'll never teach your son to be a good loser. I will, however, teach him how to lose with honor and class, because he will know that he left every ounce of his worth that day on the field and drained himself trying to help his team win."

God. Did. Not. Create. Us. To. Enjoy. Failure.

I did have a parent question me on it one time. This parent said, "I just think winning means too much to you. These boys need to explore more of football and learn to play multiple positions, and if that means losing, then so be it."

I told her, "I'll never do that. I never accept losing or

intentionally orchestrate a situation where we may lose, just so our boys can have more fun losing. Winning matters, and the reason it matters is because <u>God did not create us to enjoy failure</u>."

<u>God. Did. Not. Create. Us. To. Enjoy. Failure</u>.

Say that to yourself over and over again.

Jeremiah 8:4-5 is grounding for me. Jeremiah was urging the people to return to God, and God instructed him to say to them:

> *"Do men fall and not get up again?*
> *Does one turn away and not repent?*
> *Why then has this people, Jerusalem,*
> *Turned away in continual apostasy?*
> *They hold fast to deceit,*
> *They refuse to return."*

It's the overtone of what God is saying here that is so natural to learning to win again. In essence <u>God is telling His people that living in failure is unnatural</u>. He is telling them that they were not created to live in the emotional and relational squalor that sin ushers into a person's life.

RETURN TO THOSE THINGS YOU LEFT

Many years ago, early in my Christian faith, I read Henry Blackaby's classic work, *Experiencing God*.

It was a fresh wind to many evangelicals, and especially to my denomination, because anything reeking of "experience" was automatically cause for skepticism.

You know those pious religious leaders who saturate many churches, the ones who drink starch instead of water? Well, these are the people who seemingly have never encountered and been awestruck by the presence of God. Ironically they are the same ones who tell you that you aren't allowed to experience Him either.

Since they have no idea what it means to experience God, they believe you shouldn't be allowed to either.

Blackaby challenged that idea in a most unique way, but it worked.

And in doing so, he said in terms of experiencing the freshness of God, "Go back to where you left Him."

What were you doing back there when you felt His strength in your life? What habits were you engaged in at the time? What people surrounded you in that season? What were you watching on TV, and more importantly, what were you refusing to watch and let enter your mind?

It's interesting what David did once Nathan confronted him about his adultery. In Psalm 51 David opened up his life and let us look into the windows that exposed his spiritual journey out of the grasp of utter failure.

To start with, he <u>appealed to God's mercy.</u> That's quite wise if you ask me. It's not that God forgets anything, of course. No, it's just that we see a pattern in the Old Testament in which many times God's people call out to Him in ways that He has responded to in times past. They recall, or call up, His <u>unfailing love</u>, or they go before Him <u>praising Him</u> for <u>His great power over creation</u>.

Here, in Psalm 51:1, David said, "<u>Be gracious to me, O God...</u>"

Here's the thing: you only ask for those things you do not have.

> *If you ask God for something, you are in complete realization that you are deficient in some area of your life.*

If you ask God for something, you are in complete realization that you are deficient in some area of your life.

David asks for God to be gracious, and later he asks for God to have compassion. He knew he needed grace, for he knew his sins of murder and adultery were heavy before the Lord.

Right after that, David owned the sin: "Against You, You only, I have sinned" (Psalm 51:4). He knew that no one was to blame but himself.

Then David said something to God that lets us in on just how detached his heart had become from the very God who said of David himself, "I have found David the son of Jesse, a man after My heart" (Acts 13:22).

David requested of God: "Restore to me the joy of Your salvation and sustain me with a willing spirit" (Psalm 51:12).

A man only asks for what he does not have.

David had nothing left in his spirit. His heart was done. His song was gone. And he knew it.

David was learning that all the wild sex in the world wouldn't restore a song to the heart of a righteous man living outside the wire.

He wanted his joy back.

See, that's what the porn video never tells you. You don't get that disclaimer on the front end.

> *Sin is a taker with a heavy price to pay.*

You'll never read, *Warning: In the next ten minutes you're going to watch two gorgeous women have sex, and you're really, really going to like it, but it will eventually own you and then rob you of every good thing you have in your life right now. It's going to leave you thirsty and barren and broken eventually.*

No, you don't get that truth on the front end. You only see it for what it is in the aftermath of the carnage it causes.

Sin is a taker with a heavy price to pay. David let his heart chase the wind, and a hurricane was what he got in return.

And in that vacuum where air was absent, David lost his song of salvation.

LINKS TO WISDOM

My dad is a retired PGA professional, which means that I grew up in the game of golf. Maybe that's a core reason why I've never been afraid to get counseling at the first sign of trouble. Golfers, at least good golfers, are students of the game.

There's a known axiom in the game of golf that stands as a historical principle to guide a golfer in getting his game back on track. It comes in the form of an acronym: GAP.

Grip. Alignment. Posture.

When a man's game goes south, a solid golfer knows to return to the basics. And this is not a sign of weakness. No, in fact, great golfers are quick—very quick—to go back to square one.

Legendary gamesmen like Ben Hogan and Harvey Penick were dogmatic about assessing their grip when the ball started flying erratically. Hogan believed that grip is the key to the golf swing, because the grip is literally where a man first comes into contact with the club. If that part of the swing is tainted, it affects everything.

As for alignment, learning to check this area of my game is where I first learned the critical value of assessments and audits.

When I was a young boy, right about the time my dad was entering the PGA world, my dad was an apprentice under a Director of Golf named Gil Bettez.

Gil was truly one of a kind, the sort of man you never, ever forget.

He was raised in the North and played football for the Army in his early ears. Gil was both confident and blunt.

Gil would tell you exactly what he thought, whether you wanted to know it or not.

He was a true professional, though. He dressed nicely, took life seriously, and played to win—on every level. The saying "He's in it to win it" suited him.

Gil did nothing halfway. *Nothing.*

And Gil had a huge heart. He loved young boys and girls interested in learning the game of golf.

I didn't have to ask Gil for help. He approached me immediately when he saw that I was a young golfer who wanted to win.

I remember the very first time Gil took me to the range to assess my game. I saw him go into the club repair room and grab a can of white spray paint. I was thinking, *What in the world?*

We got to the range, and Gil took me off to the side, well off the tee box. We got away from everyone. It was then that he told me the basics of learning how to practice.

"True players, Jason, learn to work on their game, not just beat a bucket of balls. To do that, you need to get away from everyone else."

He then took the can of white spray paint and painted what would resemble a grid akin to railroad tracks:

He put my feet on one track and told me that the perpendicular line was for ball position. The first track was to align my feet to the target. The second track was to mentally see the path of the club head to the target.

It was all about alignment.

You must realize that Gil was a master teacher. Literally.

He had given lessons to some of the greatest athletes in sports, including Hall of Fame quarterbacks and PGA Tour players.

Gil would do anything, employ any tool, if it meant pulling someone out of a slump. I once saw him use a bunker rake and swing it like a sand wedge to show me how easy getting out of the sand could be if I learned the right technique. He actually did get the ball out of the bunker with a rake!

RETURNING

Finding your swing when it has left you is nearer to walking the path of a disciple than you may realize. <u>You must return</u>, for that's what a disciple does: he isn't content to live in failure. Rebuild you must, and to do it, you must go back to the fundamentals.

After his great fall with Bathsheba, <u>in the returning</u>, <u>David asked God for joy</u>. Consider this simple reality especially in terms of praying: you never ask for something you already have. David asked God for joy, because he had lost it. You can do the same thing. You can ask your great God, this Father of compassion and mercy, to give you what you do not have.

David needed a new spirit. It's interesting to me that he asked to be sustained with a willing spirit (Psalm 51:12). He knew that he did not have the power to drum up the energy to thrive anymore. He was a dehydrated man living smack in the middle of the most barren land he'd ever traversed.

He had to find a new way to live.

And for you to get a fresh start, you may have to do some new things to get some old results. I cannot tell you specifically how that will work in your life. What I can do is give you some examples of how this has worked well in my life during times when I found my walk with God to be less than stellar. When I find that my joy is fading, my song is gone, and I need to reorient my spiritual GPS, here are proven tactics that speak well to me.

Righteous Music

I have a huge affinity for music. I think I get it from both sides of my DNA. My dad was a rocker. During the 1960s he saw virtually everyone who played on a stage. Deep Purple, Grand Funk, the Rolling Stones, Janis Joplin, Jimi Hendrix—I could go on. Because of his love for classic rock, I grew up listening to those tunes every time we were in the truck. My mom was and still is a Motown fan. She also has a huge love for '70s soft rock.

So my love for music is quite schizophrenic. If you were to look at my iTunes account, you'd see the Hollies alongside Bruce Springsteen and Merle Haggard and, yes, Poco, Ambrosia, Rod Stewart, The O'Jays, Percy Sledge, the Temptations, and virtually every Motown act that accompanied that era. Then throw in that I grew up in the '80s and you've got yourself one messed-up musical database—but I love it, and you'd better check your wallet before you play me in any kind of "name that tune" game, because I'm gonna take your money, honey!

When it comes to growing in Christ, the only thing that has consistently grown my heart, other than scripture, is God's power working through music.

Whenever I find my heart stale, I discipline myself to listen only to Christian music. That works well for me.

Obviously I'm not one of those types who believe you should listen only to Christian music. Yet I do think that believers should not fill their minds with things that work against the holiness of God. So I've had to cull singers and bands over the years that perform music working against a pure heart.

However, music, to me, is a fast and proven way to set your mind on those things that are "pure" and "right." Philippians 4:8 tells us, "Whatever is true, whatever is honorable, whatever is right, whatever is pure, whatever is lovely, whatever is of good repute...dwell on these things."

Spiritual Structure

Another source of course correction for me in times of dryness is adding simple structure to my daily life. Now before you freak out at the threat of 4:00 a.m. wake-up times, wait a second, because that's not what I'm going to point toward.

I'm a very "from the hip" kind of person, so anything that

has the slightest hint of structure automatically sounds to me like micromanagement and boring results, so I run from it like a scared dog.

I'm learning that structure doesn't have to be complicated or binding. In fact, it can be quite simple and easy. The most important aspect is to do something different. Change it up.

Let me show you how this has worked for me in the past.

Many years ago I was in a deep funk with prayer. I just couldn't seem to get my mind focused on it. And I didn't want to tell anyone because I felt embarrassed that a young minister was having a hard time praying. Because, you know, I was sure that nobody else in my congregation ever struggled with praying, and I figured I'd lose my job if they knew their pastor was struggling with it.

So I decided to pray at stoplights. I know it sounds weird. Can't even begin to tell you where I came up with that idea, but I did it. I wanted to get in the habit of having my spiritual eyes open throughout the day, not just one time a day when I read scripture. So every time I hit a traffic light, I knew that I had about sixty to ninety seconds to talk to the Lord about something.

It worked. I built in the habit of watching for God to work throughout the day. Yes, it was structure. No, it was not complicated.

Don't Fight What You Can't Change

One of the greatest flaws in the spiritual structure approach is that people often work against their personality in order to find new results. Sometimes you do have to do that, for sure, but oftentimes you need not try to rewire your spiritual hard drive; what you need is to use your created design to your advantage.

I have a friend who is heavily gifted in areas of metrics and strategic operations. Like most people gifted with this mindset, he's not seen as much of a relational guy. The idea of "grip and grin" at a party gives him acid reflux.

He's the kind of guy who feels the whole world is right if he can close his door, get some work done, and never get interrupted. To him that's a super-great day. To me that's cruel and unusual punishment!

Yet that's why he's incredibly good at what he does in his career field. The problem is, he has a few people who report to him, and their greatest criticism of him as a leader was that he didn't seem approachable. His employees felt as if they were bugging him if they had a question about something.

He wanted to change his leadership style to accommodate relationships, but he didn't know how. And to be more specific, he felt awful when he found out that his teammates secretly didn't like him that much.

He wanted to learn how to honor God by loving people better, but he didn't know how.

We met for lunch one day, and I walked him through how important it was that he remove the guilt over how God had made him. God made him introverted for a reason, and he couldn't have been more "relational" even if he wanted to be, because it wasn't in his DNA. God needed him to be who he was designed to be: a systematically structured person. However, he did need to learn how to be the best version of himself, and that meant learning to value people not as interruptions, but as living, breathing souls.

Knowing that he lived and died by his calendar—that is, he scheduled everything to the quarter hour—I challenged him to use that to his advantage.

I said, "Look, man, do this. Set up one hour on Tuesday and one hour on Thursday to walk the halls, shake hands, talk about football, or just drop in on your teammates and check on them."

I told him that at first people were going to freak out and not know how to take him. However, the greatest thing he could do was to learn that interruptions were of God.

That's right. Interruptions, for him, I said, were sent from God. God was trying to teach him that people needed his amazing wisdom, and that was not an interruption: that was a gift!

The crucial thing was that he could "schedule" loving on people. Now that may seem stupid to those of us who are "people persons," but to him it wasn't stupid at all; it was revolutionary.

After three weeks he couldn't believe the difference. His team's morale saw a massive upturn. Imagine that!

Yet what my friend put into practice did not work against his personality—he employed it to his benefit.

That's a simple example of using who you already are to love God and love people better. It wasn't rocket science, but it was just creative enough to get him back to center.

Tell Your Story

If it were possible to scream and yell on paper to get your attention, I'd do it. This would be my screaming and yelling section. About all we have in the writing world is the exclamation point!

We are left with this sad excuse for intensity: !—a stick and a dot. Somebody just wasn't thinking when they created the keyboard.

My brother, if there is one place where I could force you to do something, it would be right here. I'd force you to tell your story of failure to anyone who would listen to you tell it.

We've spent a lot of time talking about a thief. Let me tell you, from years of experience, about the way he keeps stealing from you after you've failed. It's called *shame*. You feel shame for what you did. You feel embarrassed. You wish you could just move on and nobody else would ever know.

> *My brother, if there is one place where I could force you to do something, it would be right here. I'd force you to tell your story of failure to anyone who would listen to you tell it.*

I get it. I really do.

When you conceal your wounds, you also conceal the goodness of God.

No kidding, you really do. When you let shame hold you hostage, you conceal the story from those who most need to hear it.

Did God forgive you? Absolutely.

Did God restore things? Yes, He did. And while He may not have restored all of them yet, He's not done.

When you conceal the victories because of the shame,

you throw everything out of whack.

When a quarterback is interviewed after a Super Bowl victory, what does he talk about in those precious seconds? Does he go over every single time he threw a bad pass or made a bad defensive read resulting in the play falling apart? *No!*

He talks about the victory. He talks about the things that went right. Why? Because that's what champions do. They accept the failures as part of the journey. Yes, they'd love never to fail, but that's not reality. That's not life outside the wire.

<u>You must tell your story. With your head up.</u>

Here's what so many Christians never realize, and it's so very sad. What most believers never see is that their greatest ministry ventures, their most amazing stories of redemption that healed wounds for other people, their most exciting moments of serving God *never* happened because they never used their <u>pain for God's glory.</u>

They kept their pain concealed, and after the wounds healed, they just lived out the rest of their days with scars, allowing no one to see the places where the Great Physician healed the wound.

Oh, sure, they saw the healed wound. They gave personal, secret glory to the Father, but nobody else was allowed to see the victory.

That's the real shame, if you ask me.

What if, just by God's grace, you were telling your story of greed and financial mistakes over lunch one day with a buddy, never knowing he was struggling with envy and greed himself? What if, just by that one lunch, God used your story and a simple club sandwich to wake that guy up? What if his kids were able to go to college because Dad didn't squander the money on a home and a truck and a lifestyle he couldn't afford, and all of that was traced back to a time when he had lunch with you and God spoke to him through that encounter?

> *God uses your story of pain to show His redemptive glory. Don't rob God of His glory, and don't rob others of the opportunity to avoid pain and suffering just because you are ashamed of your past.*

Do you see how simply and easily that happens? God uses your story of pain to show His redemptive glory. Don't rob God of His glory, and don't rob others of the opportunity to avoid pain and suffering just because you are ashamed of your past.

You don't have to go on television. You don't have to start a website. You don't have to write a book.

Just be faithful to tell your story when the opportunity naturally arises. That's what obedience to God looks like, my brother.

8 : IN THE END. . .

I have a friend who is a famous Christian author. He's written some classics. Not long ago we both arrived at church early and saw each other in the lobby. We began to talk about writing, publishing, and upcoming projects.

I speak at men's conferences all over the nation, but my author friend speaks at international conferences and at prayer, healing, and revival services before full stadiums of people.

We were discussing the primary audience that tends to read our work, and for me, of course, that's men. He writes for Christians at large.

He elaborated, "Most of my audience is overseas." That shocked me because he is a big name here in America among believers.

As we spoke about the types of events where we speak, he said something that, for whatever reason, I've never forgotten to this day.

As we drilled down into the spiritual climate of evangelicals in American churches, he said, "You know, Jason, if I speak at a conference or assembly here in America, there might be a few hundred people at best."

Now before I go on, please realize that my author buddy is a very humble person. He wasn't disappointed in the numbers who come out to hear him speak in the United States.

> *If you're reading this book, my gut tells me you believe the devil is real.*

He then said, "But if I speak overseas, there will often be ten thousand or more people in attendance. No kidding."

I said, "Really? Wow, man. Why do you think that is?"

His answer stung: "Honestly, Jason, I really do believe it

IN THE END. . .

is simply because you don't have to convince people in other countries that the devil is real."

And there it is.

He's dead-on accurate.

If you're reading this book, my gut tells me you believe the devil is real.

BRIAN AND HIS PARTY

My buddy Brian Hinkle knows the devil is real. Just ask him. Brian saw him face-to-face—in the form of a woman.

Brian is doing better now. A ton better.

Brian has an amazing wife, Jeanine, who stuck with him through the whole ordeal. Not many women would have possessed the courage to push through the pain and find the joy she and Brian cherish today.

A few months ago my wife, Michelle, and I got a wild text from Jeanine.

She told us she was hosting a small surprise party for a few people to celebrate the one-year anniversary of the worst day of Brian's life.

As I looked at my phone, her message grabbed me.

A lot. We were definitely going to be there.

This I wanted to see.

We arrived, and five couples were there who were "in the know" on the entire situation. We were all friends, so it wasn't weird or awkward at all.

After a while Jeanine had us all gather in a circle. She said, "I know this whole idea of a one-year celebration sounds weird, really weird at first. God has done so much for me and for Brian in this past year. His grace, His mercy, His redemption. It's just surreal how good God has been through it all, and there was no way I was going to let this calendar date pass as a failure. That day was awful, but this year has been awesome. I wanted to celebrate and not let the enemy dominate this day. For on that day, what Satan meant for evil, God took and used for good."

I cried. We all did.

Tears of joy were in our eyes as we went around the circle and spoke love and admiration over Brian and Jeanine, along with praise to our great God, the Reconciler.

So here's to you, all of you, my brothers in Christ.

Here's to praying that you never have to host a party like Brian's party.

Yet if you do, go all out. Have the cake. (We did!)

Celebrate the truth that yesterday's dramatic failures do not define tomorrow's story.

You may be a wanted man, but you are *chosen* of God.

And don't ever forget it.

> *Celebrate the truth that yesterday's dramatic failures do not define tomorrow's story.*

NOTES

Introduction: You Are Being Hunted

1. Jim Collins, *Good to Great: Why Some Companies Make the Leap...and Others Don't* (New York: HarperCollins, 2001), 324.
2. Ibid., 325.

Chapter 1. Brutal Fact #1: Confront the Hunt

1. Claire Groden, "This Is How Much a 2016 Super Bowl Ad Costs," *Fortune*, August 6, 2015, http://fortune.com/2015/08/06/super-bowl-ad-cost/.

Chapter 2. Brutal Fact #2: You Live outside the Wire

1. www.GunSite.com

Chapter 3. Brutal Fact #3: The Power of Obsession

1. F. F. Bruce, *The Gospel of John* (Grand Rapids: Eerdmans, 1983), 226.

Chapter 5. Brutal Fact #5: It's Critical to Know Why You Are a Wanted Man

1. Steve Chapman, "What I Wouldn't Give" (Times & Seasons Music/BMI/Admin. by Capitol Music Group, 2002). Used by permission.

Chapter 7. Brutal Fact #6: You Must Navigate Failure and Do It with Brutal Hope

1. Jim Collins, *How the Mighty Fall* (New York: HarperCollins, 2009), 29–33.
2. Ibid., 85.

TURN THE PAGE TO READ AN EXCERPT FROM

A perfect combination of book and DVD offers a high-caliber tandem of biblical insights that will draw you closer to God, who has called you to a life that transcends complacent, run-of-the mill manhood.

Find this book and more from Shiloh Run Press
at your local bookstore or www.shilohrunpress.com

SHILOH RUN PRESS
An Imprint of Barbour Publishing, Inc.

Preface

Who knows why this book ended up in your hands? Perhaps you received it as a Christmas gift, or maybe your kids picked one up for you in hopes of fulfilling the gap on Father's Day. Many things in life seem random.

There's often something unexpected about the way God moves a man forward; at least that's my experience. I've noticed that more often than not, God moves a man forward quietly. It's odd, really. No lightning split the sky the day I came to Christ, and no thunder shook the kitchen floor the day I first thought of putting out a word of truth that a man could read in about 60 seconds. These things happened on seemingly ordinary days.

With 60 seconds in mind, I didn't put much thought into it when I gave the original series the title of *The Man Minute*. It seemed to fit decently enough, I suppose.

Very quietly thereafter, God took His normal approach of moving something forward in men. To be completely candid, I cannot explain it. I cannot explain why other projects I've launched didn't move very far, and something as seemingly random as *The Man Minute* has spanned denominations, people groups, and even oceans to get inside the souls of men of all walks of life.

I cannot attempt to explain why *The Man Minute* fell into your world, either, but it has no doubt landed on the path of your journey. I cannot tell you what's going to happen to you as you encounter scripture throughout this journey, other than to say that your life won't be the same. You're going to have God say things to you through some of these 60-second time investments—and only He will know the reasons why the words hit you the way they did.

God doesn't take part in the coincidental, and He doesn't offer random. His paths are sure and battle tested. And His words are worth slowing down long enough to encounter.

Now that our paths have crossed, my heartbeat for you is that you never rush the 60 seconds as you read *The Man Minute*, because I know from experience that God can do a lot to a man in just a minute.

Now to him who is able to do immeasurably more than all we ask or imagine, according to his power that is at work within us, to him be glory in the church and in Christ Jesus throughout all generations, for ever and ever! Amen.
EPHESIANS 3:20–21

You'll Find It (If You Really Want It)

*The Pharisees and the teachers of the law were looking
for a reason to accuse Jesus, so they watched him
closely to see if he would heal on the Sabbath.*

LUKE 6:7

If you want to see the beauty of life, you'll find ways to make it happen. The opposite is true as well. If you want to find fault in people, it's easy to do, and it won't take you long to accomplish your mission.

I know I have junk going on inside my bones. In fact, you'd be better off just coming to me and letting me tell you where my weaknesses reside. Believe me, I know where they live.

Religious leaders followed Jesus around town—not with open hearts, but rather to find any reason whatsoever to bring Him down. Jesus was without sin, but that didn't stop them. In the absence of sin, people will often create trouble for you—even if you are the Sinless One sent to redeem all humanity.

These mockers had seen Jesus' miracles, had seen love in action. That's not enough, though, when you're a religious snob. They had to find fault, or else they would have to look into the mirror.

Let us never be like those religious leaders. Let us never be the kind of people who go out of our way to find fault in others.

What *Not* to Do

Like one who takes away a garment on a
cold day, or like vinegar poured on a wound,
is one who sings songs to a heavy heart.
PROVERBS 25:20

Having spent more than 20 years in ministry, I've learned that when people's dreams are crushed or their hearts are breaking, the worst thing you can do is to play the part of the cavalier pied piper with an upbeat song. It's cold to sing songs to a troubled heart.

Don't misunderstand: the scriptures are not telling you to withhold songs of hope. People depend on hope, for the absence of hope can cause someone to follow harmful paths. Be sure to offer hope, but be careful how you package it. When people are heartbroken, the last thing they need is the guilt that comes from hearing someone say, "It's all good. Just praise the Lord anyway."

I've learned that deep despair causes people to ask questions, and those questions—when pain is too fresh for praise—tend to drown out songs of joy. What people remember most in times of heartache is that you were there. The best way you can help them is through the glorious simplicity of your presence, because that reminds them that God hasn't left them stranded.

Neglect

*"Who am I, Sovereign LORD, and what is my family,
that you have brought me this far?"*

2 SAMUEL 7:18

I recently felt the strong pressing of God's hand on my heart concerning neglect—specifically my neglect of Him. I had been letting anything, and everything, move in line ahead of Him, and I had been neglecting taking the time to have consistent conversations with the God who made me.

King David said something that will forever haunt me. God is moving among His people, and the ark of the covenant is on the move as well. David begins to have visions of building God a proper house. God shares His vision for His people through Nathan the prophet, and David is overwhelmed that he's a part of the plan.

It's then that David asks, "Who am I?"—a question that shows the king's astonishment that God would desire a man like him. It's a question I ask myself often.

We live in a world of upside-down wisdom, and it's easy to think that something could be so important that it gets priority over daily conversations with God. Yet so often I bow to that way of thinking.

I know God doesn't *need* me to talk with Him. He's not in need of anything. But for some reason, He's made me a part of His plan. Because of His wonderful, unexplainable love for me, He *wants* me to talk with Him, because He knows that my very life depends on it.

I just can't afford to neglect the time He wants to spend with me.

What You Can Become

Judas son of James, and Judas Iscariot,
who became a traitor.
LUKE 6:16

The Gospel of Luke refers to Judas as the man who "became" a traitor. Things like that can happen to a man when he isolates his heart to his own whims.

No man in his right mind just gets up one day and says to himself, "I'm going to have sex with a woman who isn't my wife." No man gets up in the morning thinking, *I think I'd like to embezzle money from my company and spend the next few years in prison.*

I'm sure if you walked up to Judas just 12 months before he betrayed Jesus and told him he would sell Jesus' whereabouts to those looking to arrest Him, he would have looked at you as though you were sent straight from the devil.

Every time I've asked someone who's had a great failure in his past about how it happened, there is always one common denominator: it didn't happen overnight. Every one of these men can point back to a specific time when things started to slip.

A man usually doesn't just *fall* into serious sin. Rather, it's often a slow descent culminating in the terrible realization that he's become something he never dreamed he could be.

Out of Options

*But when she could hide him no longer, she got a papyrus basket
for him and coated it with tar and pitch. Then she placed the
child in it and put it among the reeds along the bank of the Nile.*

Exodus 2:3

I never knew pain—real *soul* pain—until I became a father. There is something about watching your kids go through pain that takes you to places your own personal pain simply cannot take you.

Imagine the torment Moses' mother went through as she placed her *infant* child in a homemade floatable basket and released him to the fate of a river. That's desperation beyond comprehension, and it required tremendous trust in God. It was either that or have him killed—for that was the edict passed down from Pharaoh, that any Hebrew who gave birth to a boy must turn him over to be thrown into the river to drown.

Sometimes I wonder how we as the people of God treat a world that doesn't know Him at all. I wonder how we affect a doubting world when we so casually throw around the idea of "trusting God with everything."

As Jesus followers, we often reduce trusting God to a message of: "Hey, if you were a better person, a stronger person, a true believer, then you'd just trust God. It's that simple."

Okay, fine. Then go ahead and put your eight-week-old son on a homemade float and send him down the nearest river. How simple is it to trust God then?

When you encounter people who are in unthinkable situations, always tell them the truth. Tell them that trusting God is their best option. Testify to that truth, but by all means testify gently. What a person whose world is collapsing needs in that moment isn't a flippant theologian but a real friend who speaks the truth in gentleness and love.

What You Think You Need

"Which is easier: to say, 'Your sins are forgiven,' or to say, 'Get up and walk'? But I want you to know that the Son of Man has authority on earth to forgive sins." So he said to the paralyzed man, "I tell you, get up, take your mat and go home." Immediately he stood up in front of them, took what he had been lying on and went home praising God.

LUKE 5:23–25

I think Jesus intended all along to heal the paralyzed man whose friends had brought him to Him for healing. I think He saw an opportunity to address some toxic chemicals buried within the hearts of the religious elite at the scene, and He wasn't going to miss it.

Jesus showed everyone in that crowd that there are things you *think* you need, and then there are things beyond that, things God knows you *really* need.

This man probably thought his greatest need in life was to walk again—and who could blame him? If I couldn't walk, I'm sure walking would consume my thoughts every day.

However, even if this man's legs worked perfectly, sin would still paralyze his soul. Healthy legs would have simply allowed him to walk into hell on his own instead of being carried there by others.

What he needed most was not the ability to walk, but a free soul. And Jesus was more than willing to offend some religious elites to teach us that lesson.

Reckless People

*Better to meet a bear robbed of
her cubs than a fool bent on folly.*

PROVERBS 17:12

Can you imagine hiking through the woods and encountering a grizzly sow who cannot locate her cubs? The truth is, there is most likely less than a 1 percent chance you'd walk away from that encounter without suffering severe bodily harm, most likely death, at the paws of a beast that can kill not only quickly, but without remorse. You'd call any man a fool's fool to mess with a panic-stricken sow. In fact, most of us would readily admit that such a man got what was coming to him.

So put the thought of that kind of encounter into the context of Solomon's wisdom about people who live recklessly. A "fool bent on folly" is a man who has abandoned common sense and caring. He is bent, meaning the hard-wiring of his soul craves that which is no longer in alignment with the heart of God.

I've watched men become reckless. It's an ugly thing. Too many times I've heard men relay to me that they honestly believed they were immune to the depravity of those within their circle. That same thinking is akin to thinking you can encounter the panicked sow and walk away unscathed.

The wisdom behind Solomon's words is this: stay away from those who live recklessly, for if you put yourself within their circle, you will not escape without scars. Reckless people wreck people. Whether or not you think it's possible, they will take you with them to places you don't want to go.

Which Father to Listen To

*My son, keep your father's command and do not forsake your mother's
teaching. Bind them always on your heart; fasten them around
your neck. When you walk, they will guide you; when you sleep,
they will watch over you; when you awake, they will speak to you.*

PROVERBS 6:20–22

Solomon wrote of the wisdom of listening to your father and mother. But it
has occurred to me that his core message is directed at those who follow
Yahweh.

The apostle Paul called our enemy, Satan, the "father of lies." And if a
man is not in Christ, then he will listen to and follow that father, the one
who wants to sway his spirit away from his heavenly Father. The devil often disguises himself as one speaking with a voice of reason, and he often
tells men to "follow what you think is best."

Whose voice do you listen to—that of the heavenly Father, who always
has your best interests in mind, or that of the father of lies, who wants
you to do only what you want to do? If you are in Christ, then a new spirit
is in you, and you can trust your heart to hear the voice of your heavenly
Father. You are not obliged to follow what you hear or feel in the moment.
Rather, you can "bind" the teachings of your Father on your heart so that
"they will guide you."

Start with Where You're Standing Now

"You have been faithful with a few things;
I will put you in charge of many things."
MATTHEW 25:21

Envy can reveal itself in subtle forms. Envy, like every other sin, is often the starting place leading in a direction far away from God. Because sin usually starts small, you tend not to notice it so much—and something as subtle as envy feels a long way from stealing or murder.

So often when I speak at men's events, I hear men talk about how they wish they could have a place in ministry that impacts men. The truth is, they *do* have that place, but they don't recognize it.

A man will often look at what he wishes he had instead of looking at what he actually has in front of him. This is Satan's way of keeping him on the bench, entertaining thoughts of getting into the game.

My grandfather fought in World War II, and he was once assigned to a unit that, in his words, "had a lot of city boys in it." He recalled a time when the men were starving because it had been days since they'd even seen any real food. Then they pushed through some timber and entered a field in the German countryside. My grandfather's heart exhaled with relief, but one of the men lamented, "When are we ever going to find some food?" My grandfather answered, "Boys, we're standing on potatoes."

Cultivate the field you're standing in right at this moment. It's the only field God has given you for now, and He wants you to work it as hard as you can. Read between the lines of Jesus' story of faithfulness, and you'll find this important truth: God won't give you larger fields to work until you plow the ground you're standing on today.

Small Things

Every good and perfect gift is from above, coming down from the Father of the heavenly lights, who does not change like shifting shadows.
JAMES 1:17

Not long ago I was on a personal retreat—planning, praying, and just spending personal time with God. I figured that if I went to Bozeman, Montana, I'd be in the mountains—literally closer to God—and thus my spiritual reception would be stronger.

I remember getting up one morning, sitting on the steps of the cabin and enjoying the view of the mountains, and praying something like this: "God, don't let me miss You in the small things today." I had no idea what that prayer was about to do to me, in me, and around me. I soon found out.

It started with the owner of River's Edge Fly Shop spending an incredible amount of time with me, showing me some of his hot spots on the local rivers. It continued as a girl at a coffee shop—who seemed to be energized by helping others, even someone buying a single cup of coffee—treated me like a true friend.

After spending some time planning and looking into my ministry work, I was on my way to get dinner at a local dive in Bozeman. It was then that I hit a time warp that has messed with my brain to this day. I had run out of gas just once, and that was in high school. Once was enough, for I learned that living on the edge of a thin tank wasn't worth the hassle. My own vehicle is a Toyota Tundra, and when its low fuel warning light comes on, I know I have about 40 miles left. That wasn't the case with the truck I'd rented. Apparently, when the gas light came on in that vehicle, it was its way of saying, "Life is about to get painful for you if you don't find a gas station in 47 seconds."

Within 10 minutes of running out of fuel, I was in a car headed to a gas station. It was driven by a husband and wife—the Reids—who treated me as if I were their grandson in need of help as they helped me get back on the road.

When I finally got to a local restaurant, I found it was going to close in about 30 minutes. My food came fairly fast, but I basically had the place to myself. Ross, one of the attendants, approached me and asked, "What kind of music do you like?"

For some reason, at that moment I chose to say, "Classic country." He immediately changed the background music to classic country, and out came Waylon over the speakers. "You didn't have to do that," I said.

"Well, why not?" he answered, and we entered into a long conversation about how rare it is to see businesses do the small things for people nowadays.

I felt the encouragement of God surrounding me so thick that I could almost breathe it in, and just then I remembered that I had asked God to keep me from missing Him in the small things that day.

I couldn't help but wonder how many days I'd had just like this one, when so many things went my way, yet I simply couldn't see it. . .because I wasn't looking.

ABOUT THE AUTHOR

Jason Cruise is a nationally known speaker, published author in the world of men's ministry, and host of *Spring Chronicles* on the Sportsman Channel. His fingerprints are on many of the resources in publication today that engage outdoorsmen to discover strategies that connect a love for hunting with their love for God. He lives in Tennessee with his wife, Michelle, and their two boys, Cole and Tucker.

www.JasonCruise.com

Twitter: @JasonLCruise

Facebook: Facebook.com/JasonLCruise